When Heaven SHAKES THE EARTH

Extraordinary stories of everyday people

LIVING HOPE
ALOHA, OREGON

GOOD CATCH PUBLISHING

This book was written for the express purpose of conveying the love and mercy of Jesus Christ. The statements in this book are substantially true; however, names and minor details have been changed to protect people and situations from accusation or incrimination.

Published in Beaverton, Oregon, by Good Catch Publishing.
www.goodcatchpublishing.com
V1.7

Printed in the United States of America

Table of Contents

FOREWORD

We live in a generation enamored with the silver screen. What we see projected for our entertainment are adaptations and dramatizations of real life. I have read the life stories of a few great people I have known. If asked what I thought about their stories, I would be compelled to comment, "Their telling wasn't as I remembered it."

The stories of this book have not been adapted nor dramatized; they have not been exaggerated or inflated. They are stories of real people who made mistakes, had mishaps, or were themselves victims of savage forces. They are people who have endured some of life's greatest difficulty. Their report is at times raw, humbling, and heart wrenching, but above all, their reports are 100% true. These are not the stories of people seeking to polish their image to make better press; they are the stories of people who want to communicate the truth and the reality of their lives because of a great force that transformed them. Thus, the most compelling part of what you are about to read is that they are exceptional stories due to their truth. They are extraordinary stories because the miracles are real.

These people are neither idols nor icons. They live among us; they are a part of our community. We at Living Hope Fellowship commend each person whose life experiences are found on these pages and testify to their authenticity!

JESS G STRICKLAND

ACKNOWLEDGEMENTS

With much appreciation to the many people who have so graciously shared with me their stories, prayed for lost souls and put this book together, I sincerely extend my thanks to you all. The energy, commitment and love are all being reflected in this book.

To the people who's humble hearts reveal the Glory of God through their life story: Amy Scott, Brian Ashman, Chris, Chuck Bahnsen, Jamie Harris, Jeff and Sally Durr, John Watson, Julie Penn, Margaret Harris, Marie, Mara, and ZoeAnn Cook. Thank you.

To the people who took the voice recorded testimonies and used their awesome talents to write these wonderful stories: Amy Whalen, Aria Anaforian, Brianna Lindley, Cliff Brady, Julie Penn, Kim Blanquie, Maryl Smith, Nathan Lindley, Sarah Vertner, Steve Cook and Troy Sutton. Thank you.

To the editors and proofreaders who skillfully fine tuned the stories with their great understanding of the English language and beautiful writing styles: Amy Whalen, Candi Jones, Carter and Christa Cheston, David and Julie Penn, Dorothy Beaman, Kim Blanquie, Michele Snyder, Chris Durr, Sharon Ulrich, and Troy Sutton. Thank you.

To Evan Earwicker for the stunning cover design. Thank you.

To Tim Smith for all your hard work pulling this team together from the very beginning and encouraging us, aiding us and praying for us through to the very end. Thank you.

To Good Catch Publishing for the untiring and tremendous job of producing this book. It's been absolutely enjoyable working with you! Thank you.

Sincerely,

JULIE PENN

Acknowledgements

Little is done without the leadership and sacrifice of that person who is willing to step up and take the final responsibility. With that in mind I would like to personally thank Julie Penn for her tenacious spirit, her commitment to excellence and her robust faith. This book is the result of her vision and love that has impacted every page of this book. She is a quiet, godly woman with a soft smile and a never-give-up attitude — THANKS.

Finally we get to the product you have in your hand. Your eyes are presently gliding across these letters, your brain translating them into sense and then as you continue to read your life will fill with hope. Well, all of that would be a vapor of imagination without the vision, determination and dedication of my never-say-quit friend, Daren Lindley. He coached us through every step, sought to enable us to place the best product possible in your hands and then laughed, cried and rejoiced through every testimony — Bravo.

Sincerely,

JESS STRICKLAND

ONE
AMY SCOTT

Looking out my bedroom window, I felt a horrible burning sensation shooting up my back. My legs were numb. I watched the rain come down in tear shapes, hitting my bedroom window. They sounded like crystal shattering in a far-off place, a place where I wanted to be. The raindrops kept falling, turning the shattering into one long, high-pitched scream in my head. I seemed to be watching myself from somewhere far above my body. All I wanted was for the pain to go away.

In reality, it was my sheltered life that was being destroyed. After turning on the local news channel the day before, expecting to see the usual barrage of crimes by unfamiliar faces followed by the weather forecast, I was surprised when the words "Special Report" flashed on the screen. What the unsympathetic reporter said next, I will never forget.

"This just in: the murdered body of Natalie Kingston was

found in a shallow grave in the woods, one mile off the interstate, not more than three miles from her home."

"It can't be Natalie!" I thought to myself. My best friend had mysteriously gone missing just a month before and no one had seen or heard from her since. Horror, fear, shock, and dismay all congealed into one immense feeling that slammed into the pit of my stomach. Despite my initial disbelief, I knew that it was my dear friend, Natalie, but I refused to accept that truth.

"Oh my gosh, Dad! Dad, come quick!" He came running into the living room.

"Is it true, Dad? Is it true?" I screamed.

"I was just on the phone with Natalie's parents," he replied. "They found her. She'd been buried alive."

I fell to the floor. It is all I remember of that day, and it will always feel like yesterday.

Natalie and I had grown up together, from Barbie dolls and lemonade stands to driver's licenses and school dances. I felt as though I wanted to shut all the doors, close the curtains, and hide under my bed so I could feel safe again for just five minutes. It seemed to me that I would never be safe again – that at that moment even God could not protect me.

Returning to high school was lonely. Not only had I lost my closest friend, but also I felt shunned by most of my peers. In fear of saying the wrong thing, they said nothing at all. Instead of attending Homecoming, I was attending indictments, court hearings, and a funeral. Natalie's boyfriend was being held, pending charges, for her death. She was three months pregnant. Just two months prior we were picking out baby names while setting off fireworks at her mom's Fourth of July barbeque. The everyday gossip across the school hallways seemed ridiculously insignificant compared to the life and death issues I was facing.

A year later, I found myself in Washington D.C. standing before the House floor. I was there to plead justice for the lives of unborn victims. Unfortunately, the arguments between the House and the Senate surrounding this controversial issue prevented any law from being passed. I was crushed. The flight home was very long. I felt as though I had done nothing to help Natalie; nothing was effective. This seemed to be the culmination of all hopelessness and loneliness. I wandered through my junior year aimlessly.

I had the idea that emotion and stress in life could be read like a gas gauge and I had already reached the full mark. Unbelievably, I was about to experience another jolt that definitely topped off my emotional tank. I was just sitting down to dinner when the phone rang.

"Hello?" I answered.

"Amy, it's Alissa," said my one other best friend.

"Hey, what's up?"

"Uh...I'm kind of in shock. I'm still trying to come to grips with the whole thing."

"What whole thing? Alissa, what's going on?"

"I went to the doctor today and...well...I...Amy, I have Crohn's disease."

Alissa burst into tears and I remained quiet and stunned. I did not know what to say. I really wanted to break down and cry with her but I knew I could not. I had to be strong.

"Alissa, you are going to get through this and I am going to be walking right alongside you."

"Okay Amy, okay."

I had made the assumption that by avoiding the emptiness and sadness of losing Natalie everything would work itself out. Now the added stress of the probability of losing Alissa to this disease made me want to just curl up and hide from the world. In the short space of a year I had had enough bad news broken to me.

It was not long after, near the start of my senior year, that a girl named Heather befriended me. It felt nice to have a friend who did not carry a lot of baggage, as I did. She was funny and I could not remember the last time I had really laughed. We hung out after school and got to know each other well. She was seen at school as a bit of a troublemaker. I could not understand why she was so labeled but I would soon find out.

AMY SCOTT

On Halloween night, she introduced me to drugs. I smoked pot with her for the first time and entered a whole new world. Being high felt amazing to me at first and gave me a new-found way to temporarily escape all of my pain. We started smoking marijuana often, and this new path I chose was eventually a more painful road than I had already gone down. Despite doing drugs, I still maintained my grades at school. I hoped this would keep my parents and teachers from getting suspicious. It did not work as well as I had hoped because my parents knew something was going on. They could not quite put their finger on it but they knew something was wrong. I had shut down and stopped talking to them – or to anyone else for that matter. Doing drugs had led to more sin and devastation.

One night, when I had gotten very high, Heather and I entered into a sexual relationship. A few weeks into the relationship I questioned my behavior, but any ability to make rational decisions had disappeared because I was high all the time. The longer the relationship continued, the more possessive and controlling Heather became. I did not like the way I was being treated and I was living with perpetual guilt. I had been raised in the church and knew the life I was leading was not right, but at this point my longing for acceptance was greater than my conscience. I was in deep and I wanted out. Heather knew I was not happy, but every time I mentioned ending this twisted relationship she would grow angry and threaten me. She would say things like, "I will kill myself if you leave me!" Sometimes she would threaten to tell everyone about our relationship and I could not stand that. I was horrified at the thought of my parents or any of my peers finding out. I just wanted to run away but I was trapped. I started using drugs even more.

Seven long, drug-induced months later, I tried to confront Heather once more about ending our relationship. On the drive out to her house I tried to recount the steps that had led me to this mess, but I was so exhausted I could not think straight. My face was white as a ghost, my hair was long and straggly, and I had no appetite for food or for living. I just did not care what happened to me anymore. That was really the only reason I had the courage to say anything. But it was not really courage.

"Heather, I'm just going to say it. I want out. I can't be in this relationship anymore, I just can't."

"What? You don't know what you're saying right now. I know you don't really mean that."

"Yes, I do Heather, I'm not kidding around. It's over!"

Heather spent five hours trying to convince me to stay and try and work things out.

I went straight home, more wilted and brittle than a leaf left out in the hot summer sun. I had officially fallen off the edge of sanity and could not handle life anymore; I began sobbing uncontrollably. I ran into my room searching for a taste of solace but found it nowhere. Grabbing a book off my desk, I threw it as hard as I could across the room. I threw anything I could get my hands on, and then fell to the floor, physically broken down.

When my mother arrived home, I told her everything. I told her about the drugs and about being involved in a same-sex relationship. I expected her to be angry and I was so afraid she was going to reject me. Instead, she wrapped me up in her arms and held me close.

"Everything's alright now, Amy. We're going to figure this thing out," she said, lovingly.

My father was not as accepting as my mother. He wanted to punish me and he felt that he had been an inadequate father and that he must have failed me somewhere. He did not think I needed to see a counselor, but my mom pushed for it. She even threatened to divorce my father if he did not let me see one. So I was scheduled right away to see a great Christian counselor. It was the best decision my mother could have made. Things were finally starting to straighten out in my life. My father later apologized for not being there for me during my breakdown. The counseling sessions were changing me and helping me to get another step closer to living the life God intended for me to live.

One day I was in a counseling session and I had remembered back to an instance when I was doing drugs. It was around two in the morning and I was so high from the drugs, I had fallen out of

Heather's window and hurt my leg. As I was lying there on my back gazing up at the stars that night, a sudden peace came over me and I was ready to start talking. I could finally see that God had not taken Natalie from us because He was punishing me, and I also saw that He had not left me during that time – He was carrying me through it. It was in those early morning hours that I started to feel safe again. God had protected me and He protected me from serious injury that night. Someone cared for me. The concept of the Father's love seemed completely incomprehensible.

Although I was going to counseling and turning my life around, Heather still harassed me. She had become so unpredictable that they had to keep me under surveillance at school. At my graduation, Heather showed up in full military, camouflaged fatigues. She looked as though she was ready for war. It was a frightening time.

The older we get the harder it is to deal with the lessons of failure. School had ended and I poured myself into a full-time job. That made the momentary failure easier to handle. I met Mike at work. Initially, I was intrigued at having a relationship with a man. I thought to myself, "This will be great! I will just have a normal life." I felt my relationship with Mike was a way to prove to my father that I was normal and that he did not have to be weird around me.

Things were going fine with Mike until we entered into a sexual relationship. Everything started falling apart and then one morning when I arrived at Mike's house, I discovered he was cheating on me. There I was, right back where I started. I had hit bottom again. Any trust that had been built with God was broken. I was broken, and the beacon of light that had begun to shine through the black clouds of the storm was again covered. All I could see was darkness.

At the beginning of summer, I had received a full scholarship for a college in Washington D.C. and I could not see a better time than now for escape. So I ventured out to the great unknown in hopes of finding some sort of peace, and most importantly, a purpose for my depressing life. Because I did not trust anyone, I had a hard time making friends, but I decided I would do my best. I really wanted to start over and live a good life. I wanted to be a good person.

After a short time, I managed to find my way into a group of friends. However, my college friends partied and were involved in drugs, and I did not want any part of that lifestyle any longer. I was not involved with the same things my peers were, and I grew progressively lonelier. I missed my family and wanted to be there for my friend Alissa, so I made the call home. I told my mom I missed them and I was ready to come home. She gladly received me and the next thing I knew, I was on a plane headed back to Oregon.

When things finally settled down after I returned home, I started working. I went from job to job looking for something to satisfy me, yet still feeling sad and unfulfilled. What was missing in my life? I needed something; I needed love. In my pursuit to fill this incredible void I did the worst thing I could have done. I called Heather and arranged to meet up with her. Before I left for college, I had made a pact with myself to stay away from drugs and all of the things I deemed bad. I had accomplished this goal and I could not think of a better way to reward myself than to see Heather.

I knew it was foolish, but I was reaching for anything to bring some sense of peace to my disordered, chaotic life. I stumbled into drugs once more. She had marijuana and I needed to escape. I was weak and my longing for peace was immense. Our meeting also re-awakened feelings in Heather and she began pursuing me.

What had I done? I was not about to walk down that road again. There was such a pull and longing for acceptance; I needed to talk to someone but not just anyone. I needed someone who would love me but would give it to me straight. I needed Alissa. She was my most treasured friend and we had walked through every season of our lives together. She had been there since the beginning and no one understood me more. Alissa was rational and would love me the right way. I made the phone call that same day.

"Alissa, it's Amy...I've messed up...It's real bad..."

"What did you do, Amy?"

"I've blown it Alissa; I've really got myself into a jam this time."

I put everything out on the table. I told her about everything

AMY SCOTT

I was feeling. I even went back to Natalie's death and the effect it was still having on me. I told her about the longing, deep within, for acceptance and love. I told her how I could not completely break my relationship with Heather because there was something tying and drawing me to it. What Alissa said to me will ring true for all eternity; it was profound and yet so simple: "Amy, God made you a woman to love a man, not a woman, and God never makes mistakes. I am your best friend no matter what. Gay, straight, black or brown, but you know this is wrong. You need to go to church. YOU NEED JESUS!"

I needed Jesus? No way! I wanted nothing to do with God or church. I was through with trusting a God that just kept letting me down. Alissa kept inviting me every Sunday to go to church with her, and every week I would graciously decline until, finally, one Sunday I agreed, but only to shut her up.

We drove to church in silence and I reluctantly walked into the chapel. I saw men and women of all ages with hands stretched upwards singing praises to Jesus. They were singing songs about their faithful friend and Father. When I heard the voices of praise, something made me hungry for more, and I felt my heart, which felt like a ton of bricks, begin to lift from me. When I heard the rhythms of the drums an excitement was stirred inside me. I wanted to experience the freedom that I saw on the faces of those people.

From the moment I set foot in that room, an incredible and

indescribable peace covered me. I had found what I was looking for. A man stood at the front and began to speak about a God whose love is unfailing and a God who shows mercy to all men. My heart was overwhelmed. The people were very loving toward me. I realized it was not God who had messed up my life, it was I; it had happened because I put my faith and trust in all the wrong places. Here, I was finally accepted. I had found a God who did not judge me. I entered with a huge wall around my heart and a fear of being condemned, but God had a plan. He used His people to gently break down the barriers I had hidden behind for so long.

I remember the pastor talking about God's grace for all sin, yet I could not help but feel shame and guilt because of my past life, especially with what had happened with Heather. I did not deserve this incredible love and grace that was being offered. I wanted to be the person God originally intended me to be. I wanted to live a rich and full life with Jesus in the center of it. Right then I made a commitment to God. I was done with drugs, destructive relationships, and the nasty attitude I had been carrying around for years. I heard God saying to me, "Make a commitment to Me."

I kept going to church and three months later, after accepting Jesus into my heart, I met a man named Damian. I was still trying to figure out this Christian lifestyle and trying desperately to live a life that was pleasing to the Lord. I liked Damian, but he just wanted to be friends, and that was difficult for me to accept. At the time, I could not understand why he did not like me, but now I see that I was not ready. Although I had surrendered my life to Christ, I still struggled a bit. The difference this time was that every time I had a struggle, a voice would whisper sweetly in my ear, "Trust Me, Amy, trust Me." It was Jesus, my Savior. I finally reached a point where I was ready to totally surrender, so I wrote an email to Heather and completely severed all ties. What freedom! I was ready to receive whatever God had in store for me.

I heard a pastor say once that God answers every prayer with a yes, no or maybe. Well, God answered my prayer about Damian with a bright, bold yes and He did not waste any time! God was working in Damian's heart and the very next day, after I sent the email to Heather, I received a phone call from Damian asking me to be his girlfriend. We dated for over a year and we enjoyed every moment, especially the ones where we lifted our hands together in praise to our Lord at church. He shared my faith and respected me. That December he got down on one knee and asked for my hand in marriage. We were married the following February. How awesome! Jesus was only waiting for me to completely surrender my life to Him and then He blessed me with a wonderful, loving husband. I trusted Jesus to bring me joy and happiness, and He did.

Damian and I moved to Portland. We searched for several weeks, and then we found a place to call our church home: Living Hope Fellowship. When we walked in, I knew immediately this was the community God wanted us to be a part of, and He has matured us here. Our pastor, Jess Strickland, preached a sermon one day about loving without expectation. He talked about reaching out to your community and then he said something that impacted me forever. He said, "What did you do today to show love to someone?" That struck a chord in me. I knew I would never be able to evangelize about this loving Father if I did not accept that I was worthy of God's love. I was still angry and it took some time to let go. I had this new heart just waiting for me, a heart that was not self-mutilated. Through my time at Living Hope I have learned so many things, most importantly, to forgive myself.

Forgiveness is the key to life. The enemy tried to rob me of who I really was, but I now know who God says I am. I am beautifully and wonderfully made and it is only by God's miraculous grace that we are saved.

TWO
CHUCK BAHNSEN

"Give me your money, now!" I rumbled as I stuck my gun between his startled eyes. Instant recognition registered on the drug dealer's face. I had a reputation. A satisfied smile briefly twitched at the corners of my mouth. This was so easy. Without speaking, he pulled a large roll of cash out of his pocket and handed it to me, rapidly withdrawing his hand as if scalded. He knew if he were uncooperative, I would leave a bullet between his eyes without a second thought. Even worse, he might provoke a beating from the wild man towering before him. What he could not know was the source of my otherworldly rage. It baffled him because he had heard the reports... I never took the meth. All I wanted was enough cash to buy booze. I put the roll of money in my backpack and, turning my back to him, walked away. I did not care what would happen to him when he returned to his supplier with empty hands. I was scum, a predator who preyed on people who preyed on others. My only life goal was to head back home, if you could call it that, with a full bottle.

When Heaven SHAKES THE EARTH

I lived in the middle of a large field where I carefully cut and rolled back the sod over a 5 x 8 foot area. Digging down about six feet, I then created a living space slightly larger than a grave. After lining the hole with cardboard for warmth, I covered the opening with plywood and rolled the sod back into place. Anyone gazing over the field would never guess that it contained a rodent of my size. Of course, I shared the field with a multitude of normal sized rats as well. I could hear them scramble through the grass when someone walked in the field; this was my failsafe home security system. No one could come into the field without my knowing. It created the barrier of isolation that my rage required.

That dirt house was a far cry from my childhood home. I grew up in the Bay Area in a 1960s "Leave it to Beaver" home with loving parents and doting grandparents just down the street. Every day after school I would ride my bike past the houses on our block. In every home there was a cabinet filled with lovely bottles of green, brown and clear glass, bottles of a magic elixir for a middle class culture trying to escape. Alcohol was in constant use by everyone.

My first taste of liquor came from the glasses left on the table at parties. I was only six years old. By the time I reached twelve, I was talking adults into buying me beer and wine for a financial kickback. My first experiment with hashish began by stealing a pipe from a neighbor's party and sneaking behind the shed to smoke it with a friend. As he and I leaned against the wall coughing, our faces green from the harsh smoke, he said, "Man, we gotta find another way to smoke this stuff." Undaunted, I made a poor man's pipe by poking a hole in the side of a coke can. My friends and I soon began our own little stoners group. In a short time I was lovin' it! Once I stepped onto that treadmill I was not interested in slowing it down.

I began to change. When my folks said, "Chuck, don't do that!" it became my point of rebellion, my new celebrated cause. Rebellion appealed to me in a world where adrenaline ruled. One day I asked a friend, "What's next?" LSD was. One hit and I was off in a wonderland of colors all blending into an amazing, unreal movie. "Wow, I think these trips are improving my mind. I am astoundingly creative on acid!" At that same time there was a lot of cocaine going around. It quickly became my new drug of choice, a complement to the ever-present alcohol. Eventually I discovered that methamphetamine was cheaper and longer lasting than coke, so I switched to the low cost brand. But, amphetamines always bite back. During college I lost my scholarship to repeat incidents of uncontrolled rage. At age eighteen I suddenly found myself with nothing better to do than wander from bar to bar. I was unable to see the fallacy of my belief that I could not be a funny or functioning person unless I was on something. I thought I was happy and still in control.

Always looking for a new high, I tried smoking heroin and was soon "chasing the dragon." Eventually, I started injecting the heroin and began an eight-year addiction. In time, a lack of money forced me to taper off my heroin use until, over a two-year period, I completely quit. But I still had my first love, alcohol. I drank even more to compensate for the lack of drugs. I was sometimes the first one at the bar when it opened for breakfast at 6:00 a.m. and the last to leave at closing. I used to joke that my laundry cost me $60 to do because the laundromat was right next to a bar.

I got a job driving big rigs and purposed never to drink at work. Near the end of my shift I would begin to shake and become sick with delirium tremers. My self-delusion began to crumble as I faced the reality of where my choices had taken me. But the minute I punched my time card I would say, "Now it's time for dessert," then head straight for the bottle. It did not take much alcohol to cheer me up. Who cared about self-image when I was feeling better? Alcohol had been my faithful lover for over 28 years. I had no real girlfriends. My view of women was the same as my view of drugs: they were for instant gratification and then I would move on.

I lost my job to a layoff. Suddenly, I became just another alcoholic loser without any identity to give him value. Once again, I turned to drugs to numb the negative self-evaluation. I cashed in my 401(k) and the money began to rapidly disappear. I could not maintain a job because no shower was hot enough to diminish the smell of my drinking. I was a walking, pickled human being. Without the restraint of job responsibility, I got my first DUI. I began to pick fights and my uncontrolled rage eventually landed me in jail.

Chuck Bahnsen

When I was released I moved back home with my folks, dragging my surly attitude with me. I literally sneered with defiance. My own dad became afraid of me and began to keep a tire iron by the bed at night. By the winter of 1996 the welcome was worn out. I had completely pushed everyone away in my anger. "Why me?" I growled to no one in particular. "What has this stinkin' world got against me? I'm a hard worker. I deserve more! I shouldn't be treated like this! Well, I don't need 'em. I don't need anyone."

I walked away from my family and became one of the homeless on the streets of Vancouver. Tricks of the scam artist trade enabled me to survive. I stole from other homeless people and that is the lowest of the low, but the ever-present alcohol deadened the pain. When things got cold, I literally dug in for the winter and took up residence in the field. Most of the time my high security hole was tolerably warm, but when rainwater sometimes got in or when I got too cold at night, I would get up and keep moving. My gun always went with me. The alcohol created an illusion of warmth and my home was never without ample supplies of this precious heating fuel. In all, I lived in that hole for three years. My life stunk in every way.

One day I was lounging on the streets when a guy said, "Hey, some church up the road is handing out money." What did I have to lose? I wandered on over to see the nice people at City Harvest Church who were stupid enough to help someone down on their luck. I had this interesting idea that if I came across as real quiet, I might get more. The people I found there were kind, but they were weird. I was used to being looked at with fear. These people were not afraid of me at all. "Come on in and have a cup of coffee!" What planet were they from?

Every Saturday night I went into the church lobby for money. Then I began to go Sunday mornings with the excuse that people were an easier touch right after a good dose of sermon-induced guilt. I did not realize how much I was listening. I somehow felt calmer there. There was an atmosphere of peace and the rushing in my head settled down when I walked through those doors. I just could not figure it out. The only thing I could relate it to was the first time I got high.

One evening the pastor looked at me with genuine concern. "Do you think you need treatment?" Wrong question! Remember, I was the guy who was in control!

Then this small Vietnamese fellow named Kam began to seek me out and, looking up from the level of my lower shirt buttons, inquired, "How are you doing?" Even though I never acknowledged him, brushing him off like a fly that was interrupting my pandering, he always came back. One day, I was stunned to passivity when I saw him striding into my field to make a house call. He was bold. For a flicker of a moment I thought about changing, but not too seriously.

On August 29, 2001, I drank very heavily and the next morning I awoke with the usual shakes. I crawled out of my hole and sat there mentally moping about my future when, suddenly, I heard this huge voice go right through me like the vibrations on a heavy-duty subwoofer. It was unlike anything I had ever experienced. It pressed upon both of my ears. The question was succinct: "Are you through?" I knew instantly who it was. God had spoken to me. At that realization, I felt wonderful. God had spoken to *me*! I instantly knew I was through drinking. I crawled back into my hole, and for the next seven days went through a self-detoxification process. There were full bottles of alcohol right next to me and I never touched them. It was pure hell.

When Sunday dawned the day was overcast and surreal. Weakly, I crawled out of my hole and headed for a gas station bathroom to clean up. En route, I passed a laundromat. A girl who was standing in the window waved me inside. "There's a shower in the back," she quietly stated. "Here's a robe to wear while I wash your clothes." She was like an angel sent from heaven to help me clean up for the party. When the pastor saw me lumber through the doors, clean and completely sober, all he said was, "You're ready, aren't you?"

"Yes," was my simple answer. I sat down in the back of the church with Pastor Dave Schaff and Ray Farmer on either side and began to talk to Jesus. Then something astounding happened. People came up to me and gently touched my shoulders with their hands as they prayed. I felt a warm presence completely surround me and I began to cry. This tough guy morphed into 265 pounds of chewed bubblegum in the presence of genuine love. I opened the door to my heart and Jesus came into my life.

I left my hole for good the very same day. That field sure looked better without me in it. Ray Farmer took me into his home. He bought me a new pair of pants, some shirts, and underwear…real clothes! My appetite was back and I had a good breakfast. That afternoon I sat in his plush, tan easy chair and I watched my first football game without alcohol.

I was still feeling physically crummy. Ingrained wariness and internal warnings continued to flicker through my head: "Don't trust too much. Stay in control. What have you gotten into now? Be ready to bolt if you think you can't back out."

Ray knew it was important to get me help as soon as possible and he contacted a recovery ministry in Aloha, Oregon. It was connected to a church called Living Hope Fellowship. He asked if they could find me a bed. The next day he took me to work with him so I would not be alone. At 10:30 a.m. a call came on the cell phone. A bed was available for in-house treatment and everything had been arranged for funding through the state. I could barely believe it! I had mixed feelings as we crossed over the Columbia River to meet the man who oversaw the recovery house.

On the way there, Ray handed me his cell phone and quietly said, "Call your mother." I was shaking as I punched in her old number. My mother had not heard from me in a long time. She did not even know if I was alive or dead.

When she picked up the phone I blurted out, "Mom, I'm heading to rehab." I heard the phone clatter to the floor. When she picked it up again we both had a good cry.

Ray introduced me to Alan Land at a restaurant. This big, friendly guy, in his jeans and plaid flannel shirt did not look at all like what I had expected, and I hesitantly climbed into his car to head for rehab. My concept of treatment was a block-shaped building with a door six inches thick. It would also include an armful of drugs to make me cooperative. When we drove up the driveway of this perfectly normal looking home, I searched around. Where were the fences? We walked inside. Where were the hospital gowns? Alan introduced me to his wife, Char. She warmly accepted and loved me the minute I walked through the door. "You don't even know me," I thought. Alan showed me to my new room and left me alone to get oriented. I sat on the bed. It was soft – better than the ground.

On Sundays I went to City Harvest when I could get there. When I could not, I walked across the lawn to Living Hope. I generated quite a few stares. With my long hair and bushy, untrimmed beard I looked like a mountain man. I imagined people asking one another, "What is that thing?"

At the recovery house I gradually began to get acquainted with Kevin who later told me, "Man, you looked like you'd had a really hard life! I know what guys like you can be like. I didn't even want to get near you." It was not long before that all changed. I began to call him my brother. Kevin understood me and he was always willing to listen. I had been alone in that hole for three years and once I started talking I could not shut up. He sat up late with me night after night as I shared my intense guilt and grief, my fear of trust, and my hunger for hope. I wondered if my life would ever have significance; I mean, I was so dense God had to yell at me to get my attention.

Psalm 40:2 says, "He lifted me out of the slimy pit, out of the mud and mire." For me, those words are literally true. When He picked me up, I required a full-scale washing. A paraphrase of Ezekiel chapter 16 says, "You were thrown into the open field and were despised. No one looked at you with pity or compassion. Then I, God, walked by your field and saw you lying there kicking about in your filth and I said to you, 'Live!' I waited for years until you were ready to accept My love. Then I brought you out of that field, bathed you clean with water and washed all the blood from you. I put warm clothes upon your back, gave you My ring and fed you a home-cooked meal. I gave you My solemn oath forever and you became My own child."

Five months later I was contemplating a transfer from in-house treatment when the pastor's daughter, Jerushah, gave a sermon based on James 2:14. "Faith without action is worthless." I pondered those words and asked myself, "What am I going to do with my life?

Chuck Bahnsen

What good does it do if I believe, but I don't know where God is taking me?" So I prayed, "God, what do You want me to do?" As I was talking to Jesus, I looked up and the men's recovery building was framed right there in the church window. I knew immediately that I needed to stay and help. In that instant, I chose to surrender to Jesus. When I was a little kid I fought surrendering to my parents; when I was older I surrendered to drugs, and eventually I was forced to surrender to the police. It was natural for me to "assume the position." But I surrendered to Jesus for a whole different reason. This time it was a choice for something good. I knew it was going to be a bumpy ride, but I was happy.

Little by little I was given more responsibility in the men's houses. At times I argued with God, "I'm not qualified… I've been clean and sober barely one year." My mom read this quote to me over the phone. "God doesn't call the qualified. He qualifies the called."

Near the end of that first year I decided to be baptized. On the day of my baptism, when I went under the water, I suddenly found myself outside of my body looking down as the water washed over the top of me. The wave was like a giant eraser on a marker board, and I marveled as I watched my old life being swept clean. I came up out of that water a whole new man.

It will always be a miracle to me that Jesus has forgiven me. I am a reborn child of God and have been clean and sober since September 1, 2001. Now I have purpose. I have learned that, instead of watching my back and pushing the world out, I can help hurting people. I currently oversee the men's recovery house and get to watch guys – my guys – come out of their holes just as I once did. We all live and work together as we process so much incredible emotional pain. And, in the midst of it all, I have the unique privilege of helping them come to know Jesus. I tell my guys that we can either choose to be self-indulgent and drag our recovery through the mud, or celebrate God's goodness in our lives. I choose to celebrate!

THREE
JEFF AND SALLY DURR

Taking an evening walk with their toddler son in his stroller, Jeff and Sally were trying desperately to feel comfortable with one another. Conscious of the fact they were not holding hands and wondering what to talk about, it was not the typical picture of a couple who had been married for seven years.

"It's nice out tonight," Jeff said, trying to break the silence.

"Yeah, I guess, whatever," said Sally, uninterested.

"Listen, going on this walk wasn't my idea," Jeff said. "You always say you want better communication. If we're going to improve things we both have to try, okay?"

"Fine!" Sally snapped back.

"Well, I was looking over our budget again," Jeff said, "and I want you to categorize all the receipts from the past two months to help me figure out where some of the money is going."

"Jeff, I uh, well, I'm not really interested in...oh Christopher, you've lost your hat, here you go, honey," Sally said, putting the hat back on her son. She did not continue the topic of the receipts.

"So, can you do that for me, please?" Jeff begged, trying to broach a subject that Sally seemed always to avoid. "I've said it a hundred times before: If you would help out with the bills once in a while…" Jeff was interrupted.

"Can't you stop badgering me about the bills? You know I don't have anything to do with them. You have to have everything done your way," she replied, irritated.

"Look, I'm just trying to fix this marriage any way I can!" Jeff's voice got louder than he anticipated and he quickly stopped talking.

"That's how you're trying to fix this marriage? No wonder it isn't working!" shouted Sally. "You never want to talk about me, our relationship, how my day was…do you have any idea what's going on in my life these days?"

Silence prevailed for several minutes as they approached their home. They reached the top of the driveway. As Jeff started getting their son out of the stroller, a sobering thought crossed his mind. He turned to Sally and said, "You know, the way you're acting, it's almost like you're having an affair."

Sally answered simply, "I am."

This was not the first time Sally had shocked her husband. Earlier that summer she had often called Karen, her trusted friend, confiding in her about the frustration that was mounting inside.

"He ignores me, Karen, he really does. I'm sick of it," Sally said. "He cares more about his job than he cares about me."

"Sally, you've been telling me this kind of stuff for years. I'm taking a vacation to Hawaii in a couple of weeks," said Karen. "Why don't you come and stay at my place for a while. Just come, relax, get away from him and give yourself some time to think about your marriage."

Being a teacher's aide at the local high school, Sally had some free time in her day to think while her students did their assignments. She soon had formed a plan in her mind. Her goal was to get Jeff's attention. She desperately wanted to get him to change, to pay attention to her.

Sally had tired of her daily routine. She worked, picked up Christopher from daycare, went to the grocery store, made dinner, put her son to bed, and then spent the rest of the evening doing household chores. Then, worst of all, went to bed alone while Jeff would stay up late working on projects. There was little conversation at the dinner table. Any talk at all was regarding the budget, yard work, or work schedules.

After Karen left for vacation, Sally packed the car with a few extra things for herself and Christopher and then headed off to work. After picking up Chris at the end of the day, she drove to Karen's vacant condominium instead of going home. It was a bold thing to do, but in Sally's mind, desperate times called for desperate measures.

She waited until late into the evening before calling Jeff to assure him that she and Chris were fine. Sally knew Jeff would be worried when they were not there when he arrived home after work.

"But I'm not coming home tonight," she said, trying to sound brave.

"What? Why not? Where are you?" Jeff demanded, confused at what he was hearing.

"I've told you over and over, Jeff, we need counseling. You never pay attention to me. All you do is work in your office, or work on the yard or work on the car! Work! Work! Work! Never *me*, never family," Sally said, her eyes now brimming with tears. With that, she ended the call, hoping this time she had gotten through to him that she was a lonely wife.

This was not the way she envisioned her marriage to be. Sally's own parents had fought constantly and had even slept in separate bedrooms. Since she had grown up with poor marriage role models, she knew in her heart that hers was turning out wrong. Ever since Sally was a little girl, she had understood that her parent's household was not normal, and she had held tightly to a dream of having her husband be her best friend. Now, she felt like her husband did not even know she existed.

Jeff sat alone in their house, completely shocked and confused at the conversation he had just had with his wife.

"What is she talking about?" he wondered. "Look at this place! It's beautiful. Doesn't she understand that I have to work hard to get money to have a place like this? Doesn't she appreciate that I do all the yard work myself? Isn't she grateful that her car doesn't break down because I know how to keep it fixed?"

These thoughts continued to plague him that night and the next as he went to bed alone. He hardly slept.

Jeff rationalized that their marriage was fine because he had achieved the American Dream. He had a well paying job, a house, a son and a wife. He believed that these things are what help to make a good marriage. His own parents had the same kind of great lifestyle that he had made for himself and what he thought he had made for Sally.

"What am I doing wrong? *Am* I doing anything wrong?"

Sally lay on Karen's bed. She thought about her husband and the lack of attention she felt from him. There was very little communication, and seemingly no love from him. Her thoughts gave way to someone else. There was a man at work who enjoyed talking with her. He had a great sense of humor and sought her out every day just to say "Hi."

"How come Rick pays more attention to me than my own husband does? *His* wife is lucky," Sally said to herself. Her heart started to long for Rick as she became more and more distant from

Jeff.

Karen returned from Hawaii a few days later. With nowhere else to go, Sally took her son and went back home.

"Jeff, don't you see?" she said, eyes flashing. "I'm serious. I need a husband who will pay attention to me. I want you to understand that! We need marriage counseling."

He still did not get it.

"Counseling? I'm not against getting help from someone if things get really bad. But we haven't even tried to work out our problems on our own," Jeff said. "Things aren't great around here, but you're overreacting."

This was his customary way of having a conversation with his wife; telling her that she was going overboard with her desire to seek counseling, and shrugging her off.

The next day at work, Sally accepted a dinner invitation from Rick. Her feelings for him were growing stronger each time she and Jeff fought, which seemed to be every time they tried to talk to each other.

"My wife doesn't get me," Rick said. "She and I have nothing to say to each other. All we do is fight."

"That's exactly how my relationship is with *my* husband," Sally sympathized.

The conversation centered on the struggles they had with

their spouses, and they found they had much in common. The more Sally talked about her problems, the more her emotions were confirmed that she was indeed sad and lonely. The very person she thought would be her best friend, her confidant, her loving husband, was not satisfying any of her needs. Therefore, the evening progressed, ending with the first of many goodnight kisses.

Realizing that her emotional relationship with Rick had turned into a physical one, she suggested to her husband that they go for a walk to try to smooth out their unhappy state of life together.

Admitting that she was seeing someone else was a relief to Sally as the weight of the secret was exposed. Nevertheless, a mixed emotion of relief and desperation clouded her judgment as she decided to move in with Rick and leave her son behind.

As she pursued the new relationship and moved into an apartment with Rick, Sally found herself in a very different lifestyle. Drug and alcohol use became an important part of the relationship. Being high masked her conscience, so substance abuse was prominent.

Because Rick had left his wife and kids to move in with Sally, the two reinforced each other's actions every day. The memories of her life with Jeff started to become dim and she assured herself that she was doing the right thing.

"How could this be wrong when it feels so good?" she reasoned. "Rick is the husband I've been longing for. He pays attention to me, we have fun, and he loves me!"

Having his wife leave him and Christopher was much more painful the second time around. Jeff began to feel bitter and his heart became hardened toward his wife.

"Fine!" he thought. "She wants to go? Go! She's the one losing a great house, family, and stability."

Jeff did not know where Sally was or how to contact her. He sought support from his friends and both his and her family. Sally's mother was supportive of Jeff because she disapproved of her daughter's behavior. This was a quite a change for Jeff. Ever since they had been married, he had often felt like the black sheep of the family.

Sally's mother had become a Christian after her daughter had moved out and gotten married. Seeing Jeff's pain and knowing that God had the answer to his problems, she invited him to church. After several invitations, he accepted.

Jeff had grown up in a Christian family, so returning to church seemed natural to him. As a child, he had attended youth group, gone to church camp, and when he was thirteen years old, he had even accepted Christ into his heart. However, he realized now that he had never actually committed his life to following God. Throughout college, he had ignored any sense that God was with him or calling to him. But he felt it now. Jeff felt God calling to him and he found it comforting to be sitting in church every Sunday.

Jeff's thoughts were overrun with questions about the next

step. Should the credit cards be canceled? What about Christopher? The last thing Jeff would allow was some other man raising his son. He would fight for Chris. One evening Sally called Jeff to check on Christopher. Jeff took the opportunity to set a new direction.

"Please meet me downtown Wednesday at 1:00," Jeff insisted. "I've scheduled an appointment for the two of us to see a lawyer about a divorce."

"Oh! Well, sure. That's fine," Sally said, slightly alarmed. Had it come to this point? A divorce? No. She did not believe it. She jotted down the information and agreed to meet him.

Sally was dumbfounded when, after the meeting, it seemed Jeff was serious about a divorce. She knew she had no right to be angry; after all, she was the one who had left her family. In her muddled thinking, this separation, this affair, was never meant to be permanent.

"We were eventually going to get back together, weren't we?" Sally asked.

"How in the world could you ask that?" Jeff asked, confused. "Don't you realize the state of this marriage? You're sleeping with someone else!"

That afternoon, Sally went back to her apartment to resume her new way of life. The one that once seemed so appealing and satisfying now started to feel ugly and shameful.

"Drugs…alcohol…sex…how have these things become a priority to me?" Sally wondered.

Sadness filled her heart as she realized what she was doing. She grieved for the pain she understood she was causing her husband.

Jeff went back to his house, once so comfortable and routine, which now felt stark and void of life. Where was his friend, his wife? Where was his happy family?

"Is this how Sally felt?" Jeff wondered, thinking back to all of her comments about loneliness.

Sadness filled his heart with the realization of his own shortcomings as a husband. He worried about where his wife was and what she was doing.

The Sunday following their meeting with the lawyer, Jeff went to church as usual. He sat in the chair next to his mother-in-law and reflected on his situation. He thought about his nice house, his cars, his job, and his yard – all the things that were once so important to him.

"All that stuff doesn't really matter," he realized. "Nothing matters anymore." His wife was gone, and he knew that if they divorced, Sally would probably get custody of Christopher. He was at risk of losing his son if the courts favored the mother. The house that had been so important to him no longer had any value. He had nothing, nothing in his life!

JEFF AND SALLY DURR

Little did he know that his wife was paralleling these feelings. Sally sat in the living room at the apartment as she watched Rick pack his things. He was going back to his wife. Rick had moved into her life with such compassion and understanding, and left her in an instant, so callously, without looking back.

Now it was Sally's turn to think about what she had in her life: nothing. No boyfriend, an apartment with a few of the bare necessities, no husband – nothing! She felt desperation stronger now than it ever had been.

She got down on her knees and cried out, "NOW WHAT?" Because she was not in the habit of praying and had never considered asking God what to do before, she was not sure to whom she was talking.

Then, unexpectedly, she heard a response, "Go back to your husband." She did not understand who was speaking, but Sally figured that she had best obey. She quickly dressed and got into her car.

Tears filled her eyes as she thought about who spoke to her.

"Was that you, God?"

Without even realizing it, she found herself in the parking lot of the church she knew her mother attended.

"What am I doing here?" she wondered. Inside the church, Jeff was in tears; tears he had not shed once since his wife left him, but that now came unabashedly. The pastor of the church was talking about the love of Jesus and the peace that comes from committing one's life to Him. Peace was something Jeff knew he needed. Acknowledging the existence of God is very different from leaning on Him in an everyday way of life. Jeff became very aware that he had lived his adult life the way he wanted to, without listening to God at all.

When the pastor offered a few minutes for anyone to come forward to give their life to God, Jeff stepped up and made the commitment wholeheartedly. The peace he was missing and longing for instantly filled his soul.

Minutes after the service had ended, with people mingling around, and tears still fresh on his face, something caught his eye. A side entrance door opened and a bright light made him strain to see a figure standing in the corner of the sanctuary. That figure was familiar to him...it was Sally! It was his wife! The sun had lit up behind her making her appear almost angelic. Jeff stood up and Sally immediately noticed him. They walked towards each other and embraced.

"I'm coming home," Sally said when they stood face to face. They hugged each other so hard it seemed they would never let each other go.

That evening, back in their home together, they talked for hours about the past weeks and how they had felt without each other. When Sally told Jeff about the voice she had heard while she was alone in her apartment, Jeff took the opportunity to tell her about the decision he had made earlier that day to give his life to God.

"It's amazing, Sally. I heard a similar voice calling me back to church. I felt God's presence there and I can feel Him right now. I know we can rebuild our marriage and be happy if we both have God in our lives." Jeff smiled lovingly at his wife, with new hope in his heart.

There in the living room of their home, Sally received Jesus into her life. Jeff led her to Christ, using the same prayer the pastor had spoken earlier that day. Sally was overcome with the feelings of love and peace as she gave her life over to God.

Together, Sally and Jeff began attending church with Sally's mother. One day during a service, the pastor invited everyone who wanted to be baptized to come to a class that night.

"I think we should both be baptized," Sally whispered.

Jeff nodded his head in agreement.

Jeff and Sally went to that class with excitement. They later confirmed that the lives they surrendered to Jesus were His, cleansed of sin, and ready to hear God as they were baptized in the Living Water.

As the years unfolded, another son and a daughter were added to their family. Communication has become a key part of their relationship and God is always factored into everything they do. Their conversations, the movies they watch, the activities they pursue are all based on the fact that God is now the center of their marriage. They changed their expectations of each other and, at the same time, committed themselves to learning their respective roles as husband and wife. Jeff and Sally give God the full credit for saving their marriage and bringing them to a place of true happiness in their lives. Their primary focus in life has been raising their three children to know and love God.

On their tenth anniversary, Jeff gave Sally a small piece of rope made with three strands.

"This rope symbolizes our marriage. One strand represents you, one strand represents me, and the third strand represents God. If God has an equal share in our marriage, we will hold strong."

FOUR
JOHN WATSON

A large, burly guard put his hand on my shoulder. "Excuse me sir, I need to talk to you about some tapes you have in your coat." As he escorted me to the back of the store, I thought only of my father. At sixteen years of age, I was afraid he would kill me.

The evidence of my crime was in my coat. I even had a list of all the tapes I had planned to steal. The list proved my crime was premeditated. The quantity was large enough to charge me with burglary and send me to juvenile detention, but I knew I was in for something far worse.

"Your mom and dad are coming to pick you up, son," the officer told me, not knowing how terrified I was of my dad.

When my dad arrived to pick me up, he was silent. He said nothing as we drove home. He said nothing as we walked into our house. Then he shoved me aside and walked into my room. First, my stereo flew through the doorway, crashing against the opposite wall.

Next, large pieces of furniture came hurling by. Everything I had was tossed out that day, except for my bed, my dresser, and my clothes. Each time he exited through the doorway, he backhanded me with his tightly clinched fist. The last time he exited, I flinched, expecting another blow.

"You wanna flinch?" he yelled. "You wanna flinch? I'll give you a reason to flinch!" With full force, he thrust his fist into my stomach. I doubled over, unable to utter a sound. Then, grabbing the top of my collar, he threw me with all of his strength through the window and into the bushes below. I staggered back inside, covered with shards of glass.

"Are you trying to kill me? Do you want me dead?" I asked.

"You are a loser. Get out of my sight."

I caught a glimpse of myself in the mirror. Blood trickled down the side of my face.

"Oh, geez. You really did it this time. You tried to kill me. Oh, geez," I cried.

My father never touched me again.

My dad was an angry man. His first marriage ended during his tour in Vietnam when my mother abandoned me to my grandparents until my father's return. His second marriage ended when he beat our dog so severely with a hose that my stepmother left him. Like the dog, I learned to live in fear of my dad.

John Watson

Dad's third marriage lasted for nine years. Linda had three boys from a previous marriage, but had custody of only one; he was 3 months younger than me. We were brothers in name only.

We lived in the middle of the Mojave Desert, a hundred miles from Las Vegas. Our parents both worked long hours and commuted two hours each day, so we always came home to an empty house. We fended for ourselves.

The brawls I had with my brother were frequent and ugly. Worse, my father's abuse, combined with my own rage and fear, created in me a highly combustible mix. I feared I was becoming like my dad.

One day I threw a knife at my brother. Fortunately, I had just enough control to wait until he ducked behind the pool table. The blade flew over his head and dug deep into the sheetrock. We both stared as the handle vibrated.

"I'm going to tell your dad," he finally said. His jaw was tight. I knew he was really scared. "You are a psycho. Get some help, jerk!"

"You're the jerk," I retorted. "And if you tell, I'm *really* going to get you."

"Well, you almost *did*. Look at the hole in the wall." We both looked at it. The room got quiet.

"I'm sorry," I said finally. "I don't know what came over

me." I thought about what could have happened. "I am really sorry."

A different time, earlier in my youth, when my brother would not give me any room while I tried to line up a pool shot, I shoved him out of the way and broke the cue in half. Unfortunately, my dad happened to glance up from his paper at just the wrong moment.

"So you think it's funny to beat people with sticks," my father said, as he rose to his feet.

"I wasn't trying to beat him," I said. "He wouldn't get out of the way." It did not matter what I said, though. My dad began to rage.

"What's with you, John? Someone gets in your way and you use a stick on them?"

"Dad…I said it was an accident."

"Maybe *you* should be the one to feel the stick. You think you're such a big man, don't you? I'll show you a big man…"

"How come you never get mad at *him*? He's the one who started it," I yelled. My brother glared at me from the other side of the table.

Then, my dad used the long slender half of the pool cue to beat me. The broken pool cue was his weapon of choice for the next several months until it broke from frequent use. Then he switched to the large handle end, which he had kept. As hard as it might be to believe, my father's beatings became so frequent that they finally began to lose effect.

Summers were different though, because I often went to visit my grandparents. They had a wonderful home on the Sacramento Delta. Their RV backed right up to the edge of the water with a deck out back. I remember sleeping outside on an air mattress, listening as the water lapped up against the dock. I loved the warmth of summer and the smell of the night air. The wind played gently with the hanging chimes.

My grandparents always made sure everybody felt loved. When I was with them, *I* felt loved. I remember going to church with them and watching them worship. Their love for God was contagious. When I was with my grandparents, I felt a hunger to know God better. Those summers were so peaceful and joyous. Every morning brought fishing, crawdad hunting, skiing and swimming. However, the greatest joy of every summer was their company.

Under their influence, a funny thing happened. Somehow, I became aware that I was making bad choices in my life, but I did not know how to change myself. Even though I actually had many good influences in my life and even went to Christian schools, my thoughts always returned to my angry, disappointed father and the complete emptiness of our home.

When I was 13, my step mom's second son, John, came to live with us and with him came Black Sabbath, AC/DC and Led

Zepplin. This music was new to me; it glorified being bad. Suddenly, it was as though I had found a whole new way to exist. Whereas before I was a troubled kid who wanted to change, now I felt pride in the trouble I caused.

During my freshman year, my dad divorced my step mom. After I went to live with him, I spent the majority of school hours off campus drinking with friends. Twice I got suspended because I got drunk on campus. I told myself that booze was better than drugs. In my mind, I was much more together than the drug crowd I hung out with. My senior year ended with my father getting divorced again.

As if the tape-stealing incident was not bad enough, my life changed forever when my father learned I had stolen from his safe. I had just finished running a track meet and my father met me in the parking lot with his new wife.

"Give me your house key," he demanded. Hesitantly, I relinquished it.

"Don't ever bother coming home. If you wanna steal from me, you can live somewhere else!"

"I…I've got nowhere to go," I stammered.

"You should have thought about that before you stole from me. How low can you go?" Dad shook his head in disgust. Then he left me in the parking lot with nothing but my running shorts and a t-shirt. With no place to go, no foundation and little going for me, I needed to find something fast.

John Watson

What happens to a young man who straddles two different worlds? What happens to a young man who runs on the track team by day and parties all night? It says in the Bible that no man can serve two masters; he will end up loving one and hating the other.

I signed up for delayed enlistment in the Navy. I had to finish my term in college before I could join, but once it was over, I was theirs. So, in true partying fashion, I coasted through the rest of the winter term, and headed for basic training.

Aside from the haircut, basic training did not prove much of a struggle. I was in great shape from being on the college track team. After basic, I went to electronics school for two years and participated in the drill team where I met a girl.

When she became pregnant, I did not know what to do.

"I don't want to be a dad at 19! I've got my whole life in front of me."

"John, it's not the end of the world. It's a baby. We can *do* this," she said.

"You're nuts. You'll have to drop out of school and my career will be over before it even starts. I wish this had never happened."

"Well, it did happen," she said. "You are looking at this all wrong."

"You are the one who needs a reality check. You're ruining

our lives." My young, beautiful girlfriend looked at me in disbelief. I do not think she had ever seen this side of me, but I was only beginning. "Have an operation," I said.

"You mean an abortion? I can't believe you want to kill our baby," she said miserably.

"It's not a baby. It's nothing yet. Look, it's no big deal."

After much convincing, I finally persuaded her to go through with it. I knew it was the wrong thing to do, but in my mind it solved everything.

Shortly after the abortion, we decided to get married. A month before I graduated, my wife moved to Norfolk to secure an apartment and get settled in.

My ship was at Todd shipyard in New Orleans, Louisiana. When I arrived, Mardi Gras was in full swing. Since my wife was not around, I decided to enjoy the local scene of New Orleans with the men of the gunnery division on the *Radford*, my newly assigned ship. I remember the first two days of Mardi Gras; I drank everything in sight. Then I blacked out.

Two days later, I came back to consciousness with the dull roar of the most forceful hangover I had ever experienced. I lay in the gutter, my head resting on the curb, groggily pulling myself to my feet. Glancing around, I saw that the city was back to normal. People were on their way to work. Workers cleaned the garbage of ten days of partying off the streets.

When I returned to my men at the *Radford*, they cheered and congratulated me. We quickly developed an affinity built around the thought, "How debauched can we possibly become?" For the next nine months, my life was consumed with alcohol.

When the *Radford* was ordered back to Norfolk, I saw my wife again.

"These are the separation papers," she said. She handed me an envelope and took a step backwards.

"Separation papers? We've barely been married." I could feel my temperature rising.

"I've been seeing someone and I'm pregnant. It's not yours." I was speechless. It was as if she had thrown a brick at me. "Don't bother coming home," she continued. With that she turned and walked off the ship.

I never saw her again. My marriage was doomed before it even began. I was crushed and livid at the same time. How could she do this to me? For nine months, I sent her my checks so she could have a nice life. All the while, she cheated on me and used my money to do it!

I contacted a lawyer, a financial hit-woman, intent on getting her for everything she was worth. She was successful at her job and I squeezed every last dime out of my ex-wife. Not satisfied with mere financial revenge, I purposely dragged my feet through the divorce process to make sure her baby was born with my last name on the birth certificate. One day, I wanted her child to look at the birth certificate and know she was the product of her mother's infidelity.

Destruction and hatred consumed me and my life fell apart. I lost everything and gave myself over to depravity. I slept with strangers and drank myself into oblivion. Even though it was I who pursued these actions, in my mind, I thought they were pursuing me.

At our homeport in Norfolk, our favorite heavy metal bar was the On Stage. In anxious anticipation of our nightly binge, my buddy, Mike, and I got off shift and headed straight for the On Stage. The buzzes progressively diminished through the weeks, as my body adapted to the immense levels of alcohol. I stopped at the liquor store on the way to pick up a pint of 180-proof Everclear. The small print at the bottom of the label said, "Warning: Causes blindness and death."

"Wow!" I said with a laugh. "This stuff must be intense!" That night, I managed to drink the whole pint. Next thing I remember after the blackout was waking up in my car drenched in a severe sweat. Wrestling against my inebriated state, I managed to open the door. I felt the fresh, cool rain wash over my body as I fumbled and crawled out of the car and fell onto the parking lot pavement. The relief did not last long. The police spotted me and immediately called Shore Patrol to bring me back to the ship.

When I came to, the misery was indescribable. I vomited for half a day. Just when I thought the worst had passed, the sickness returned with alarming magnitude. I collapsed at the toilet, and vomited continuously for several minutes. My friends, Mike and Bubba, followed me in.

"I don't like the look of this," Bubba said.

"This is worse than any hangover I've ever seen," said Mike.

I let go of the toilet and lay against the wall. I felt myself drift into a bizarre, coma-like state. I could not see anything. I could not respond to my friends.

"He's stopped breathing," I heard Mike tell Bubba. "We've gotta get 'im outta the stall."

"John? C'mon buddy. Don't leave us," Bubba said. I could not respond, lucky just to be alive. Somehow, Mike and Bubba managed to rescue me from the bathroom cell. They put me back in my rack and watched me for the rest of that day until they were sure I would recover. After that, I was physically unable to drink for several years. Even the faintest smell of alcohol would turn my stomach. I abstained for the rest of my military career.

About the time of my discharge from the Navy, the electronics industry got red hot. I easily landed a well-paying job with Intel as a vendor technician. My self-induced revulsion of alcohol had worn off. However, I was never able to get drunk again. Now I needed money to fill the ever-present void in my life. I threw myself into my work, frequently putting in 80 to 100 hours a week and pulling in six figures a year. My boss and I had a contest of material acquisition and sexual conquest.

The receptionist at the company introduced me to her niece, a beautiful and tomboyish woman named Carmen. Although Carmen and I did not hit it off right away, my friends liked her, so she became increasingly involved in my social circle. Eventually, we discovered there was more going on between us than we had originally thought and after several months of dating, I proposed. There was a friendship between us of incredible depth.

Early in our marriage, we decided to attend church together. It was amazing how God changed us. We began to spend time with a friend of mine named David. David and his wife were Christians. They were such loving people. We knew God had given them to us to help us in our spiritual walk and they became close spiritual mentors. David always talked to me about my "vertical alignment."

"You have to put God first," he said insistently, "God, your wife, your kids, then your job."

"I don't know if the boss will like your vertical alignment," I quipped.

"It's not a laughing matter," David said gravely. "If you don't put God first, your life will fall apart. You have to put God first."

I knew he was right. Carmen was already upset about my long hours and continual absences from home. Acting on his warning, I transferred to an engineering position. It was less demanding and did not require travel. But shortly after the transfer, I lost my job.

JOHN WATSON

I got another job right away but since it was only half the money I had been making, we could no longer afford to live in the Bay Area. Carmen and I decided to move to Las Vegas. There was plenty of work there and the cost of living was much cheaper.

Promptly, I landed a job installing security systems in casinos. But as hard as we looked, Carmen and I could never find a church like the one we had left in California. As we went from church to church seeking a spiritual family, slowly but noticeably our hearts began to desire the things we thought we had overcome: drinking, partying, and money.

One day at work, I got word that Intel was in town hiring technicians to work in Beaverton, Oregon. I went in for an interview and was hired, so we relocated. The job was great, but we still needed a church to attend. After fervent inquiry, one of Carmen's coworkers told us about a great church called Living Hope Fellowship. Desperately wanting to find a church that fit us, we decided to try it. It was the first church we attended after our move to Oregon.

The first Sunday we attended Living Hope, it felt like we had come home. Before we sat down, two other couples came to greet us. They sat by us during the service and afterwards invited us out to eat. We knew them for less than two hours and already we felt like we had new best friends. The atmosphere, the pastor, the music – all of it fitted us perfectly. It was just what we were looking for and exactly what we needed. We *were* home.

Through my church family and through an ever-deepening faith in God, I now believe that God has a plan for my life. I have allowed Him to shape my character and change my heart. He has also given me the desire and the ability to heal the long-damaged relationship with my father. My dad is now one of my closest friends. What a gift he is to me!

Through prayer and because I have accepted God's forgiveness, the Lord has also removed the heavy load of guilt and shame I carried with me for my part in the abortion of my child. I know I have been forgiven for that, and for every sinful choice I have made. With God, *all* things are possible.

Now I look back on my life and I can see that Jesus was there all along offering me hope, joy and peace. Today, Carmen and I have received these gifts, and we choose each day to walk closely with Him.

FIVE
MARA

I momentarily froze, paralyzed with terror as I watched her pick up the gun and carelessly wave it about while she stumbled through the house. Oblivious to my presence, Mandy drunkenly continued to weave from room to room.

"What's the point? Why am I even alive? Why?" she slurred through the haze of alcohol. She stumbled, and then collapsed, sobbing on the floor as my sense of helplessness mounted. "Today would have been our anniversary, Brad. Why did you leave me? I love you. Don't you know I can't live without you?"

I did not know how to help. I was just a thirteen-year-old who had transferred all of my starved, emotional needs onto this unlikely surrogate mother. Appointed by my father and his cult, Mandy had been my guide, teacher and virtual mother since early grade school. For two weeks, I had stayed by her side in a sincere effort to help her cope after Brad left, but now there was nothing left in me to give. Unendurable pressure and fear surged up like a volcano and shattered my thin veneer of control. The sudden force of it twisted my sympathy into a new form. I erupted into anger.

"Why can't you just get over him? He was a jerk!" My thoughts rushed about in my head in agonized confusion. "What about me? You're supposed to be there for me!" Before I realized what I was doing, I wrenched the gun from her hand and retrieved a bullet from storage. I resolutely slid the smooth cylinder into the gun's chamber then shoved the gun back into her hands.

"If you're going to do it, just get it over with. I'm sick and tired of your weak whining!" I slammed the door in frustration as I left the house.

That night she put the gun to her head and pulled the trigger. My life seemed to come to an end as well. I could not find relief for my guilt over her death. Mandy was my only anchor to security and acceptance, and now she was gone.

That night I vowed I would never trust anyone again.

Trust was a very fragile thread in the two worlds in which I grew up. I did not choose either world. Like any child, I was born into them and I made the best out of what life had handed me.

One of my worlds was the public life that was carefully constructed by my family. In public, I was expected to show exemplary behavior and high societal accomplishments. The other world was far from public. It was a secret world, deeply steeped in occultism and only known about by the select elite. I had to be perfect in public so the other world would remain unseen by those outside the circle.

My hidden world had very different rules from my public life. The contrast was mind jarring. The occult life consisted of extreme experiences, both incredibly beautiful and horrifyingly evil. Each extreme experience required rigid management of the emotions. The process of teaching these disciplines would appear inhumane to an outside observer. Even so, to a child raised in that paradigm, the lessons were necessary for survival, and all pain deserved.

One lesson in managing fear and pain left a deep, lasting impact on me. In first grade, I had the misfortune to be stung by a bee at school and I was so "emotionally undisciplined" that I had cried. When I came home, my father opened the kitchen cupboard and retrieved a glass. He then went outside to the clover in the lawn and trapped several bees in the upended glass.

"Sit here on my lap," he said to me with a calm firmness. I quickly obeyed. Then he set the cup on my leg, trapping the bees inside. "Hold it here and don't move, don't react and don't make a noise."

I sat there silently, and squinted back tears as the bees stung me continually from inside the glass.

"You need to manage your fear and the pain. Let it pass through you, then turn and look it squarely in the eyes and you will be the master. Make it serve you."

This was a needed lesson, even at such a young age, so I

would be able to repress and reshape my emotions for their proper use, most likely during ceremonies. In his own paradigm, my father was being a good teacher so I would succeed. Generations of his family had used these techniques. I glanced up at his face and searched for a gentle hint of fatherly love. As usual, his face was devoid of emotion. I soon came to think of this void of emotions as "the nothing" on his face.

My young mind was constantly haunted by fear of failure to meet the exacting demands of life. Because I suffered extreme abuse of all kinds, I rarely experienced life as safe. One evening, I foolishly spoke out of turn. I would have to be punished. Under the house was a large concrete room with a heavy cast iron door in the floor. I obediently climbed down the ladder and then turned my face up to watch the last thin thread of light disappear as the door was lowered into place. I knew from experience that I was too little to push it open. I would have to wait until someone let me out. I sat curled into a ball to conserve warmth and waited in the dark, never moving far from the door. The cold from the floor made me ache, but I was afraid to move in the dark. I sat staring, wide-eyed, at the blackness while my ears strained to catch any telltale rustling of evil things that might lurk there. The next thing I remember is being awakened in the tunnel to the rasping sound of the seal being opened. Painful light poured down on me.

My father's voice called out from far away, "Mara, come

MARA

here." But I could not respond. I was too weak to make any effort toward the ladder. The shadow of my father descended and I felt him lift me with his strong arms. I looked up into his face, lit by the dusty beam of light that poured down from above. For a flicker of a second I thought I saw compassion in his eyes. Then "the nothing" slid over his face and emptied his features of emotion. In that one clarifying moment, I was sure that I would never be loved.

One weary day when I was nine, I wandered off on our acreage and climbed onto the largest branch of a very ancient gnarled tree. I wrapped my arms around the thick trunk and instantly felt safe with the tree. Suddenly, I began to cry. I clung desperately to its side and sobbed, "Help me, would you? Please!" I did not know exactly to whom I was calling, but it seemed as if the tree responded by gently soaking up all of my pain and then sending it down its roots and away into the earth. I sat there motionless, with my damp cheek pressed against its rough side while the rosy sun began to set beyond the horizon. Then silently, a loving presence came and softly blanketed me with comfort and acceptance. I knew this presence was not the tree. Somehow, I knew that it was whoever had made the tree and I returned there repeatedly for that unconditional love. It was the only place I felt safe to express uninhibited emotion. There, I could cry and release hurt without fear of repercussion. I wondered if the tree was my guiding spirit or some ancient dryad whose waning magic had rooted it to the earth. All I really knew was that it took on my enormous pain and its solid strength always held fast. On several occasions I hid pieces of the tree's bark in my cheek to feel safe. This tree was my deepest secret...my personal sacred place.

Shortly before my thirteenth birthday my family sold our land. I was devastated by the loss of my tree and quickly transferred all of my emotional needs onto Mandy. Mandy was a part of our circle and even though her treatment of me was abusive, I loved her. She was familiar and predictable.

One early example of our relationship happened when I was instructed to memorize a specific passage so I could speak the words in a very precise manner during a ceremony. When it came time for me to recite the passage, I said it incorrectly.

My punishment was swift. Mandy stripped me down and immersed my tiny body in an ice-cold bathtub while I trembled uncontrollably. After a dangerously long time in the freezing water she lifted me out. I was barely coherent. She rolled me tightly into an electric blanket. I could not move and Mandy left me in the torturously hot blanket to sweat and cry all through the night. In the morning, she unwrapped me. Completely dehydrated and exhausted, I sat limply at the table and she brought me a glass of cold milk.

"Drink up," she said and smiled at me warmly. I remember thinking that she was the kindest, most beautiful woman I had ever seen. I loved her for that glass of milk. Although I had sustained horrific abuse, somehow I believed that I deserved it and that it was

MARA

normal. She became my angel of mercy when she brought me that glass of milk. I thought of Mandy as my safest refuge over the ensuing years.

The day I handed her the loaded gun, I walked an agonizingly long distance back to my house. The more steps I took, the more conflicted I felt. I knew I had hurt her, but I was too stubborn to turn back. The phone rang before dawn with the news that Mandy was dead.

My dad turned to me and demanded, "What happened over there? What did you do?" I could not answer him. Even though he sharply questioned me over and over, I was too traumatized to speak.

Our circle had connections. We were notified when potentially exposing or incriminating situations would arise. Mandy kept ceremonial materials hidden in a secret compartment in her home and they would have to be removed. I knew where she kept them and was brought along to assist in retrieving them.

I will never forget when we stepped into her bedroom. Mandy was half draped across the bed in the yellow lamplight. A spray of blood and human debris fanned out from the place where part of her face was blown away. Irked by my stony silence, my father turned to me and said, "See what you've done!"

I was not allowed to attend Mandy's funeral that week. I coped by latching onto my anger at her for leaving me and I made my vow never to trust again. I never cried for her. I had been trained too well.

My training or my vow did not deter God's love. At school the following spring, I was reading in the cafeteria, when I heard an uncontrollable laughter coming from across the room. The infectious roar caught up every person who sat at that table. Curious, I looked up from my book. The more I watched this joyous group, the more I noticed that they did not seem to be aware of social classes. There were popular kids and not so popular kids and everybody seemed comfortable and accepted. A few days later, I decided to loiter around their table to talk and find out about them. Oh no! They were all Jesus people!

My curiosity was thicker than my walls. One guy lent me a book about Jesus. From the moment I began to read, I could not put it down. His character fascinated me, but I could not get past that terrible part about His death on a cross. I did not understand how atonement by blood was anything different from what I had already seen in our occult rituals.

Deep inside, I was touched by His love. It sounded like a fairytale. Could that kind of love be real? Tentatively, I knelt down on the hard tile of our family room floor and prayed just to see what would happen.

"Jesus, if you are real, let me know." Immediately, I was surrounded by a sweet, familiar presence. I had felt this before! The same presence comforted me at the foot of my childhood tree. I cried softly. It had found me again. Only this time I knew the presence was a person. It was Jesus, and His love was not dependent upon my performance or my ability to stay in control. It was only dependent upon His sacrifice when He took my punishment upon Himself. God knew long ago that this was the only way I could ever understand the cross. He paved the way to my heart when I was still a child. Now, I wrapped my arms around the wood of the cross and discovered that my grief and sorrows were once more borne away and replaced with the sweetness of His love. I believed.

I fell crazy in love with this amazing God and bought the biggest Bible I could find, reading it from cover to cover. Forgiveness was a gift of such amazing magnitude and I drank of it very deeply. I could not leave the occult world at that time because the risks were too great, but somehow I trusted that if my outside life was lived with sincerity and purity, God's grace would cover my other existence.

I dove into Christianity with a tenacity I had never known. I prayed and worshipped with a joy that had never accompanied my occult path working, and began to witness at every opportunity.

The following year, my faith was shattered. I offered a ride home to someone I had met during a church meeting. He directed me to a dead-end road at gunpoint, then beat and raped me. Years later I learned that this same man had been previously incarcerated for the death of another woman. Suddenly, the violence that belonged in the occult world had invaded the safe reality of my Christian world.

At the time I could not understand why God had not rescued me, and my old fears took control again. I believed I was destined to be hurt, and I renewed my vow never to trust again…certainly not Christians and definitely not God. Instead, I turned to drugs and high-risk behavior to cope with the pain. At the same time, I pursued academic achievement in a vain attempt to reclaim some self-worth.

The most destructive of all, I plunged deeply into the occult world with renewed vigor. The hook of occultism cuts very deep. I found being admitted into a high-level group replaced the abuse, fear and deprivation of my childhood with new acceptance, beauty and affection. The relief of belonging was profound and the trauma bonding was so intense that I believed I would never leave this special world where I belonged. I hungrily grabbed onto the various theologies. They gave glorified meaning to the ceremonial acts. My conscience desperately needed this alternative morality to cope with the things I did.

Instead of expected security, I began to crumble emotionally. I had known God, experienced Him, felt Him and nothing I tried seemed to replace Him. I participated in more than six independent occult groups, some of them international in scope, and never found sweetness that was comparable to Jesus. So I resolutely moved toward a life devoid of feelings.

One day I discovered I was pregnant. Immediately, I went into hiding. My own childhood told me what awaited this child. I could not relive that part of my life again. It took two weeks for my occult group to find me.

I felt trapped and confused. I was in it so deeply, that I truly believed that the only way I could protect my child was to abort. I had to do it before anyone discovered my condition. At the time, I thought it was the most merciful thing I could do. The irony is that it was an act of love, but it destroyed something in me. After my abortion, the hard shell that protected me from experiencing emotion was gone. I could no longer ignore my pain.

Not much later, I went to a concert and bumped into a Christian brother whom I had known from my Christian coffee house days.

"Do you want to hang out sometime?" he asked.

"Doesn't he know that I'm the proverbial bad girl?" I thought to myself. I was certain that rumors of my backslidden life were well rehearsed in Christian circles. I expected he would whip out his big, black Bible and bring it crashing down with judgment on me. I agreed to go anyway and mentally braced myself to deliver a verbal backlash or a good theological argument, whichever would disarm him most effectively.

The judgment never came. Instead, he just loved me without any expectations. We spent the afternoon together playing guitar and talking about Jesus. As I sat there and talked with him, I began to feel that sweet presence surrounding us. It was just outside of my reach!

It was Jesus! He was always seeking me, no matter where I was in my life. Before long, I ached to be in His familiar comforting presence. I was so close. With my broken shell, I took a huge risk and confessed my need to this brother. He prayed with me. That night, as the evening stars sang with joy, I returned to the arms of the God who is love.

From that day forward my transformation began. Healing has not always come without pain. A broken bone that has healed improperly must first be re-broken by the good physician in order that it can be set right. Only then can a person run with abandon. Jesus is a very good doctor.

It was five months before I could completely quit my drug use. It was many more years before I could emotionally face the effects of my occult life and allow my heart to be healed. Ephesians chapter five says, "It is a shame to talk of the things that are done in darkness, but when you bring them openly to the light of Christ you can see them for what they really are." The light I thought I had through invocation and path working was only a mind full of darkness, a dreamy illusion of substance. Then Jesus arose in my heart and proclaimed, "Awake from your sleep. Get up from this dead life and I will be your light."

I married the wonderful man who prayed with me that night. Thus began the journey of learning to trust the love of Jesus through another person. It has not always been easy to trust broken believers with my own broken heart. But Christ loves to use broken vessels, not perfect ones.

I have discovered that the healing ointment most often flows from the cracks in His vessels. Love does not always come in the package that I wish or even in the form that I am looking for. Trusting still feels like a risk at times. I have learned that when I take the risk and let His ointment touch my heart, the sweet scent of Jesus pours over me through others. When I take risks, I learn that I *am* loved and that I can trust again.

As marred as my own vessel has been by life's bashings, not a crack has been wasted. I have had countless opportunities to pour out His goodness. I am able to love on the most rejected and desperate of people. I can do this because I know in my spirit that they are never beyond the reach of His miraculous forgiveness.

Jesus said, "He who has been forgiven much, loves much." I experience the truth of those words every day.

It was at the base of a tree in an ancient garden called Eden that man first fled from a life with God by eating of knowledge, both evil and good. Try as he might, he could not make his choice work. Like me, he needed a savior. I find it beautifully poetic that, at the base of a tree, God reclaimed my heart once again with the sweet presence of Jesus. I am among all people, most richly blessed.

Six
Marie

"Marie, go check on your little brother!" my mother said for the second time, growing increasingly impatient with me. As a 14-year-old, the responsibility of watching over my little brother was often given to me.

"Okay, okay," I replied, as I scampered out of the kitchen. My little brother, Guy, was only three at the time and loved to play on the front grass near the goats. As I shut the front door behind me, I began to look for the mischievous little toddler, but he was not in any of his usual play spots. My heart skipped a beat.

"Oh Lord," I whispered under my breath, and quickened my pace.

"What are you doing, Marie?" my dad asked as I hurried by. He was showing one of our horses to a potential buyer, which normally required all of his attention.

"I can't find Guy, Dad… I can't find Guy!" I hollered. I told him I had searched the barn, the goat pasture, and even under the crack in the porch, but I could not find him anywhere. Instantaneously, my dad took off running toward a ditch at the edge of our property. Then screams erupted.

"Marie! Get down here!" Dad yelled. I ran as fast as I could, my lungs pounding through my chest. "Hurry, Marie!" I could not make my legs move any faster; I could not get there soon enough. My dad stood beside a dammed stream at the bottom of the ditch, holding Guy's limp body. He had fallen into the water and now he was not breathing. I was the only one who knew CPR, so immediately I jumped down and attempted to revive him. His body was warm and wet but Guy was not responding. Growing more anxious, Dad ran to the house, got the car and came back to grab him from me; I followed right behind them. We jumped in the car and I desperately continued CPR as we sped toward the doctor's house, but there was no trace of life.

Finally, we swerved to a halt in front of the doctor's home and Dad rushed Guy inside, but it was all in vain. The doctor did a quick examination. "I'm afraid it's too late," he said solemnly.

"B-but his...his body, he's still warm!" I cried out, distraught. He said nothing. I could not accept it. "Feel him, HE'S STILL WARM!" I screamed.

"I'm sorry," was all he said.

I was born in 1927 and grew up on the farmlands of Ore-

MARIE

gon. Childhood was not always pleasant, but at least I survived, which is more than I can say for some of my loved ones. My father was severely abusive to my older brother, treating him like one of the farm animals, and taking the excess of his anger out on my older sister and me. The smallest aggravation or imperfection in our work would light his fuse, and none of us wanted to be there when it went off. He never touched my mom, however. She made it clear to him that if ever he laid a hand on her, she would leave. Why she did not protect the rest of us as stubbornly as she did herself, I will never know.

We were all expected to help with the upkeep of our farm. Fearful of the consequences that would result if we did not, we all worked hard to do our part. One evening, five years before my brother drowned, my older sister, Frances, went down to a lower pasture to retrieve some of the cows. After she was gone for a considerable amount of time, my mother, with her usual intuition, began to worry. "Go see about Frances, Marie," she said in her firm tone. At the top of the hill, I continued through the gate, staggering and sliding down the steep, wet grass that led to the pasture. I saw her there, buckled down on her knees and clutching her stomach. Worry consumed me instantly. Running to her I shouted, "Frances! What's wrong? Are you all right?"

With a twinge on her face she replied, "It's my stomach. It hurts so badly I can't move!"

"Stay here, I'll go get someone!"

"No, Marie! You can't! You know how mad Mom and Dad would be if they knew I was sick. Just stay with me for a bit. The last time this happened it went away after I kept still for awhile; so I'm sure it'll pass." Unable to do anything else, I held her hand tightly while waiting with her, and then helped her back to the house. Frances' stomach pains occurred more frequently and more severely, but still I kept quiet. Because the pain had steadily grown, my mother heard Frances when she cried out one night. The next morning, Frances was taken to the hospital. Our doctor suspected that it was appendicitis although, to this day, I do not know exactly what it was.

My parents had recently become members of the Christian Science church at the influence of other family members. Therefore, shortly after Frances was admitted to the hospital, my mother called our cousin, a Christian Science practitioner. We paid her to come pray for my sister, in accordance with that doctrine. Yet the prayers did not help and her condition worsened. As a little girl, this had an unsettling effect on me; I vowed never to become a member of any such organization.

Finally, they performed surgery. Afterwards, Frances was moved to a convalescent home and confined to her bed. I was not allowed to see her, but a friend later told me that during one visit Frances remarked, "They're going to let me die. They're just going to let me die." Frances only lived for one month after the surgery. I sat on the front porch of the home and watched strangers carry her body out on a stretcher. A deep responsibility for her death consumed me. I should have said something before her illness escalated to the point of hospitalization! I was the one who let her die. The guilt was overwhelming.

Years passed, and I had grown into a young woman by my senior year in high school when I met my first husband, Roy. He was an incredibly charming man. We were married on Christmas day, and because I was married in the middle of the school year, I was not allowed to finish high school. In those days, married women simply did not attend school. Roy was an amazing husband, and we were so in love; sharing our life together was all that seemed to matter. We had one child, and Roy worked as a news photographer at a large company. The job required us to move several times. I grew continually more homesick so, with the news of my second pregnancy, we decided to relocate closer to my family.

It was evident that Roy was much more familiar with God than I was. I knew Roy prayed for me frequently, but this divine connection also showed in the special way he treated me. He was always sure to send me flowers when we were apart, write a special note to remind me that he loved me, or buy me a souvenir when he was away on business. Roy was a gift from God, and though we never spoke of spiritual things, I knew he possessed something that I did not.

Once Roy had healed completely from a war injury he received during World War II, he bought one of the infamous Harley Davidson motorcycles. The first time he came riding up to the house on it, anxiety gripped me. The mere sight of that beast made me nervous. My husband was very protective, however, and would not have me ride it until after the baby was born.

One night, with the last ray of sunshine just hidden behind the surrounding hills, Roy and I were headed home from town on the Harley. Our boys, the oldest two years and the baby now six weeks, were home with their grandma. I straddled the motorcycle behind Roy, my arms clutched around his waist, and my hands gripping his jacket so tightly that my knuckles were white. The law did not require helmets at that time, so we rode unprotected; I wore only a scarf to keep my hair in place. Soon we had left the paved asphalt of the main highway and turned onto the unstable, fenced, gravel roads that led home. As we came around a sharp corner, I noticed an open gate and there stood horses in the road not more than twenty feet in front of us!

"ROY!" I screamed, but it was not soon enough. He swerved the bike, running into the side of the horse, and then— everything went black. When I awoke, the horses were gone and Roy was at least ten feet from me. Despite the severe pain I felt, I crawled over to him.

"Are you okay?" I cried out. Blood was foaming at his lips. "Say something to me, Roy!" He said nothing, lying incoherently, unaware of my existence. Before I could think of what to do, someone had stopped to help and I was on my way to the hospital.

I lay in the hospital bed with one worried thought racing through my mind, "Where is Roy?" I could hear the doctors outside my room explain my condition to the rest of my family. Many questions were asked that I could not quite distinguish, and I did not care to pay close attention. That is, until a response came that I was not expecting to hear. "Just send him to the morgue," the doctor said, unaware that I was listening.

"NOOO!" I cried out as dread ripped through my chest. Heads turned suddenly, realizing the unceremonious means in which I had learned of Roy's death. "It can't be true! No! NO!" I went on a rampage, sobbing until it hurt, emptying my soul. I quivered and shook, and then I simply could not move. My family's attempts at comforting me were useless. Roy was my life, my joy, the father of my children, the love of my life. He valued me over any other! He was gone.

"I want to die," I said to my mom one day while still in the hospital recovering from some broken bones and jaw surgery.

"You can't, Marie. This is no time to be selfish with your life. You have two little boys who need you." It sounded harsh, but it was exactly what I needed to hear. Thinking about my boys kept me going, moment by moment. It was time to recover and move on the best I could.

For the next two years I worked and took care of my children. I was lonely much of the time when I finally met Gary. Soon after we began dating, I learned that I was pregnant. This rushed us into engagement, and within a month, we were married. Although we probably would have gotten married anyway, being pregnant was not how I wanted to start the tone of our marriage. I felt completely irresponsible. The ongoing havoc in my life now had me wading neck-deep in residual and ever-increasing guilt. Gary was a good man, despite our hardships, and it was because of his mother that I would later be able to recover from the mountain of guilt I carried.

Two years into our marriage, our relationship was still rocky. My dear mother-in-law told us often that she was praying for us. She seemed to sense some turmoil in my life and asked the pastor of her church to come and visit me. He was very patient as he spoke with true conviction about Jesus and His ability to save me. I was desperate enough to know that I needed to be saved. During one of these visits, the pastor said something that stunned me.

"He's already forgiven you for anything you've ever done," he said. Right away, memories of the deaths of my younger brother, my sister, and Roy, as well as my unwed pregnancy, flooded my mind. "It could all be absolved?" I thought to myself. Right there in my living room, the pastor prayed with me. I asked Jesus to come live in me, and I received the forgiveness I so desperately needed.

Shortly after, I began attending a local church. I did my

best to raise and teach my children, but there was immense stress in what was left of my marriage. It seemed as if I was only able to maintain the status quo.

One Sunday morning, about ten years later, I sat in church with the heaviness of life's difficulties weighing me down. As I listened to the sermon, Jesus performed a miracle in me. Without warning, the enormous burden that was upon my life was lifted from me! It felt like my head had been taken off my shoulders! I was beset with emotion and began to sob uncontrollably. It was as though a deep, penetrating wave had come over me and washed me clean. Every ounce of shame, responsibility and guilt for the deaths, the pregnancy, and my marriage problems, was gone! Years of torment lifted in one miraculous moment; God had touched me. I cried for hours, releasing every hurt. Though it was not a fix-all for pain, I knew that I had a hope in the midst of any circumstance, and that nothing on earth would ever defeat my spirit.

In the weeks to come, I could not stay away from church. I wanted to help in any way possible. I was so in love with this Jesus who had set me free from such tremendous pain, that I wanted to do all I could for Him. Almost instantly, my marriage began to improve. It was a lasting change, progressing through every trial and struggle that Gary and I would endure. In spite of this wonderful growth, the biggest test of my faith was still to come, another ten years later.

David, my older son, had fought in Vietnam and come back

to the States. He married and had two children. David knew God and had been doing very well in life, but then started experiencing problems in his marriage. One morning, a loud pounding on the front door surprised me. I ran to the window and peeked out the curtain. There stood David holding one child under each arm. I quickly opened the door to find him soaked with rain. His car was in the driveway full of his belongings.

"David, what are you doing here? And with the children!" I exclaimed.

"Mom, please, let me stay with you, just for a little while. I brought everything with me that I think she'd destroy!" he said with exasperation.

"David, please just try to make your marriage work! Go home to your wife," I tried to encourage him. However, David would not open up to me about his marriage. He stayed with us for two days, and then returned home. Had I known what was really going on, I would certainly have given different advice. It was not until much later that I discovered my daughter-in-law's deep involvement in dealing drugs. I remember vividly a comment David made one of the last times I saw him, but I did not understand the implications: "I'm going to find them and I'm going to get them."

My son stopped contacting me and was soon considered a "missing person". The police began an exhaustive search for David, but hour after hour, day after day, our hope of ever finding him

MARIE

dwindled. One night, I woke up sweating and panting; I knew that something terrifying had happened. I got out of bed, knelt down, and began to pray. "Jesus, please! Show me where my boy is." I was expecting to hear the name of a town; instead, I saw a picture. It was a small river lined with fir trees; a very serene image, but I knew it was not entirely peaceful.

At once, my husband and I began searching every place where David had friends, or even acquaintances, but no one had seen him. As we looked, in the back of my mind, I held onto the image of the forested river area, and constantly kept my eyes open, but we never found it. We searched for weeks until we had nowhere left to go.

On the sixth week David was found. Two fishermen saw his body, bound together with rope, floating in a small river. He had been tied to a weight and thrown into the water where he would have eventually floated into a larger river. If he had, he would never have been found. Nonetheless, the weight had fallen off the rope at the confluence of the two rivers, and his body floated to the surface.

It was immediately determined a homicide. Two weeks after the funeral, I inquired of the police how they were proceeding, only to find out that they had lost all records of the murder. I was devastated beyond belief. My first-born son, my baby, was murdered, and there would be no justice. Although every inch of me wanted to shriek at God, "It isn't fair! Why did this have to happen? Where is the justice?" I knew deeply in my heart that God is just, and I felt a reassuring peace come over me. Even though I was completely confounded and did not understand why it all happened, I became calm inside. I knew that life would not be pain-free, and God would walk with me through all of it. He was close to me, giving me His comfort; and I knew I could trust that His plan was better than my understanding.

This is my testimony of God's grace – not that He eliminates my pain or makes the circumstances of my life more comfortable, but that He stays with me, gives me peace, removes my guilt, forgives my wrongs and makes my walk through life steady. Throughout the years, God has brought even more healing to my heart. For instance, I once had a dream that David and Roy sat together in heaven, looking as they had during the last weeks of their lives. They were laughing, smiling, and talking to each other. It brought me unbelievable joy to see that Roy knew his son, and to see that David was free of the strain he bore here on earth. When I woke up, I cried with relief, and a piece of my broken heart was healed.

Another day, I was in prayer at church when a memory came to me of my little brother drowning. I began to relive this memory frame by frame, and could feel myself breathing heavily as I ran to Guy's aid in the ditch. Suddenly, I had a vision; on the edge of the grass a gate had been left open, and that was how my little brother had gotten out of the yard. The responsibility I'd been carrying with me all these years vanished! I was not entirely to blame for his death! Another piece of my broken heart was healed.

Now I am 77 years old and still in love with the same Jesus I met long ago when I learned of His forgiveness. Of course, it is still painful for me to relive the memories of death and guilt from my past, but it brings me unspeakable joy to be reminded that God was there and took care of me. He healed my hurt and continues to heal my heart. Jesus is my Comforter, Forgiver and Healer—with Him I am complete.

Seven
Brian Ashman

It was a typical day at Jennifer Ashman's home daycare. She looked around her. There were toys in every corner of the house and she could hear the melodious laughter of "her kids" as they played.

"Soon there'll be one more to look after," she thought with a warm smile, as the phone rang in the next room.

"Hello?"

"Hello, Mrs. Ashman?"

"Yes, who is this?"

"This is the doctor's office. I have the results of your latest blood test."

Jennifer's grip tightened slightly on the phone. This was her first baby and every bit of the experience was met with excitement and a slight bit of apprehension.

"Yes?"

"I'm afraid that the tests show there is an extremely high

risk that your baby has Down's syndrome."

The words hit Jennifer like a slap.

"Mrs. Ashman?"

"Yes, I'm here…"

"You should schedule an ultrasound, so we can verify the results." Before making the appointment, though, Jennifer called me.

"Brian," she said. "Our baby has Down's syndrome."

I am not going to lie. When Jennifer told me the news, it was a big disappointment. It is not the kind of news anybody would ever want to hear about their baby's well being. Still, I was filled with a remarkable sense of peace. Somehow, I knew it was going to work out. I never once felt depressed or overwhelmed by the challenges ahead.

"God will prepare us for whatever we will go through. If our baby has Down's syndrome, we're still going to love him."

As we prepared ourselves for the ultrasound, we were encouraged to learn that several of our friends who had children had also tested high for Down's syndrome, but the indications turned out to be false positives. In their cases, the ultrasounds showed there was nothing wrong at all. For us, however, it was a different story altogether. After the ultrasound, the doctors told us that they had found a condition called Cystic Hygroma.

"Cystic Hy…" I paused.

"Hygroma," said the doctor. "It's a small sack of fluid that collects in the neck."

"Is it fatal?"

"It can be. It is common in babies with Down's syndrome, but more importantly, it is an indication that something is abnormal in the development of your baby."

"What are our options?"

"Have you considered terminating the pregnancy?"

We both answered without hesitation. "That is not an option."

"Very well, then. I think the next step should be an amniocentesis."

I saw a barely perceptible flinch from Jennifer. To say that she does not like needles is putting it mildly, not to mention, an amniocentesis could hurt the baby or even cause a miscarriage.

"We'll be able to get more specific information about what the problem is," the doctor continued, "and that will allow us to make better choices about where to deliver your baby."

I looked over at Jennifer. "I'll be there with you. We can do this."

The procedure was quick, a little painful for Jennifer, but the results were well worth the effort. The chromosomal analysis proved our baby did not have Down's syndrome. The doctor was still cautious, though, because of the Cystic Hygroma that he had seen in the ultrasound. In any case, we were elated with the good news.

Over the course of the pregnancy, several more ultrasounds were done to check on our baby's condition. Things seemed to be going well, but I had an uneasy feeling that there was something that the doctors were not telling us. I remember thinking that maybe it was because we asked not to know the gender of the baby before it was born. I did not dwell on it too much because everything else seemed to be okay.

We had support from our church. We could feel the prayers of our family and friends, for us and for our baby. Some people believe that God does not do miracles in the modern day world, but I can assure you that He does. If you were to see the small but vigilant group of people who prayed for us and our unborn child day after day, you would know the hands of God were at work in our lives.

At 25 weeks, Jennifer started to have contractions, and our doctor wanted her to come into the office. I was installing our new microwave oven.

"Do you want me to go?" I asked.

"No, I guess not," she replied. That was the answer I was hoping for. This did not sound like it was that serious.

However, 45 minutes later, the phone rang.

"It's Jennifer. They're admitting me."

"What? Why?"

"The contractions are too early, and they're way too strong. They have to be stopped," she said.

The drug used to stop premature contractions is called Magnesium Sulfate. It is a powerful drug that relaxes the uterus so that it stops contracting. It also relaxes all of the other muscles in your body, to the point where it is hard to function normally. After two days on the drug, Jennifer was unable to walk or even stand up, but finally the contractions had stopped.

"Is it worth it?" I asked her.

She smiled peacefully and said, "Anything for our baby."

Four uneventful weeks passed. We went back to the doctor's office for a scheduled visit at 29 weeks. A familiar scene unfolded.

"You're having contractions again. We need to get you to the hospital right away."

The doctor's office was right next to the hospital, so it was a quick trip across the parking lot, and then she was back on the Magnesium Sulfate.

But this time things were different. After two days of contractions, the powerful drug was wearing Jennifer out. After three days, Jennifer looked half dead, and was completely drained. And at four days, the contractions stopped.

Our doctor said, "You need to think about what you want to

do if the contractions start up again after we take Jennifer off of the Magnesium Sulfate. A normal pregnancy is 40 weeks. You are at 30 weeks."

"What are our options?" I asked, and I thought about what he said the last time I had asked that question.

"If we take her off the medication, and the contractions start again, we can put her back on the muscle relaxant, but it will put her in the same condition that she is now." Considering the state that Jennifer was in, I did not like the sound of that.

"Or, we can let nature take its course."

Translation: let the baby be born and deal with the complications of a premature birth.

It was a decision that I did not want to make, but sometimes what you need to do takes precedence over what you want to do. Jennifer was taken off of the Magnesium Sulfate, and later that day, her contractions began again. It was time for a decision and, fortunately, we did not have to make our decision alone.

"Precious Heavenly Father, we humble ourselves in Your presence. Lord, we come before You with heavy hearts, and a difficult decision to make. Lord Jesus, we pray that in all that we do, we will do Your will above all. We pray for the healing and sustaining power of the Holy Spirit to be upon us. Father, we know You are here with us, and in that we rejoice. We pray these things in Jesus' name, Amen."

Because of the complications, our baby was to be born by a Cesarean Section. For Jennifer, that meant two things: a spinal tap and more needles. I tried to reassure her, just as I had done during the amniocentesis.

"I'll be there for you. You will be okay. I'll be there."

As they rolled Jennifer into the operating room, they asked me to wait outside while they got things ready. Suddenly, I realized I was *not* going to be there like I had promised! They were doing the spinal tap without me! Unfortunately, there was nothing I could do, because the procedure had already begun. After scrubbing up, and waiting through the longest ten minutes of my life, they finally let me in.

The room was very cold. It looked like an unlikely place for a baby to come into the world. Jennifer lay on the operating table, with only her head and shoulders exposed to the frigid air. The rest of her was covered in blue surgical cloth. I could see she was nervous. I sat down next to her, and took her hand in mine. Standing up, I could just barely see what was happening on the other side of the drapes. I had never seen an operation before, and I was more than a little curious about what was going on.

One of the nurses saw my enthusiasm and said, "You need to calm your wife." I could tell by her tone that I was not going to see much of what was going on, so I sat back down.

Jennifer said, "I'm scared." She was talking faster than normal, with an anxious tone in her voice.

"I know. I'm here. It'll be oka—"

Just then I saw amniotic fluid flying everywhere. It hit the operating room floor with an audible splash. It covered the feet of the surgeons. One of them said something that you don't ever want to hear in an operating room: "Whoa."

"Talk to me," Jennifer whispered. I was at a loss for words.

Then something amazing happened. From within the cold of the operating room, came a little bit of warmth. From the mess and undeniable gore that is part of giving birth, came a small glimpse of heaven.

From my wife…came my son, Spencer.

He greeted the world in the same way that many boys do; Spencer peed. I could not contain myself.

"It's a boy! It's a boy! And he peed!!" In that moment, the hardships and troubles of the previous weeks melted away. I was a dad now, and Spencer was my son. The fact that he was born ten weeks too early did not seem to matter. The uncertainties of the early blood tests did not seem to matter. Nothing mattered, because the Lord had given us a son!

The very moment was a gift unlike any other. It was a gift I will always treasure in the sacred part of my heart.

However, all too soon, the sacred moments of life passed by.

Immediately, they took Spencer to the Neonatal Intensive Care Unit, or NICU. For the next five days his world was on top of a silver cart with locking wheels, a heat lamp, and a blanket to warm him. I watched as they inserted a tube into his mouth and down into his chest so that he could breathe.

There were temperature probes all over him. You could tell from the commotion that highly trained people were doing their assigned tasks and performing their sterile choreography on him. His tiny, naked body fought for life.

"It's worse than we expected," a nurse said.

"When do you think he'll be able to come home?" I asked.

"His lungs are grossly underdeveloped."

"How long will he be here?"

"I'm sorry. It's just too early to know for sure."

As Jennifer recovered from the surgery, I introduced Spencer to his family, one at a time. Only two family members were allowed in the NICU at any one time. I explained to them what this or that tube was for, and what all the machines did.

The most important machine was the respirator that supplied his tiny lungs with oxygen. Because his lungs were so underdeveloped, he could not breathe on his own, although he was trying. At times, he seemed to fight against the very machine that was keeping him alive. They finally gave him a drug to paralyze his lungs so he would not convulse against the machine. That concerned me. It seemed like a step in the wrong direction.

Later that day, the doctor told us that Spencer had Noonan's syndrome. He told us about the physical characteristics of Noonan's, and that his mental capacity would probably be affected. This was the hardest thing for me to hear. I had always done exceptionally well in school and hoped for the same for Spencer. Still, I knew that God had a plan for Spencer, and I was fully committed to my son.

"Will we be able to go home soon?" I asked.

The doctor looked at me intently and said, "We really need to take this day by day." I knew then that this was probably going to be a long-term situation. We began to see the respirator as the key indicator of Spencer's progress. If they could turn it down and eventually turn it off, Spencer would breathe on his own, and then we would know that everything would be okay.

But every day was a struggle. On his second day, he stopped urinating. It is funny how we do not even think about urinating in our daily lives, but it is a critical bodily function and without it we die. They gave Spencer a drug to make him start urinating, and it worked. It was a small victory, but a victory nonetheless.

On the third day, Jennifer had recovered enough from the operation to go home. But home held no comfort, so we went to dinner with our parents. When we returned, there was a message on the answering machine to call the doctor right away.

"We took an X-ray of Spencer, and he has started bleeding from the brain," said the doctor. There are three levels of this kind of bleeding, and he is at level one. If we can get it stopped at this point, everything will likely be fine."

"We'll be right there."

There is nothing that can prepare you for news like that. We spent the third night in the NICU.

"I'm glad we're here," said Jennifer.

"Me too," I said. "It's good to be here with Spencer again."

On the fourth day, one of the doctors met us in the NICU.

"I'm afraid the bleeding in Spencer's brain has gotten worse. We would have to say that he is now categorized as level two."

"What exactly does that mean?" we asked.

"With the loss of blood, there is also a loss of oxygen to the brain. This causes brain damage that is permanent. If he were to survive, his quality of life would be impaired."

There was a slight pause. I had a feeling there was more.

"Is the damage severe enough that you would recommend removing the life support systems?" I asked.

The doctor simply said, "Yes."

In a way, I knew that this decision was coming. The indications were there, even though I did not want to think about them.

Now we were faced with a life or death decision for our precious son that we had barely gotten to know.

As with all things, we asked God for guidance and wisdom. We met with our pastor and our family. Was this the right thing to do? Were we taking the situation out of God's hands and putting it into our own? Was it even my job to make this decision? On the other hand, the doctors were saying that it was unquestionably the right thing to do.

It was the hardest decision we had ever faced.

The NICU always seems colder than it should. And that night it was particularly quiet. My footfalls sounded like loud knocks on a wooden door as I walked over to Spencer's bed. I needed to see him. I needed to talk to him.

"Hi Spencer. How are you doing?"

I could see his little chest rising and falling in time with the breathing machine.

"I just wanted to tell you…" Tears cascaded over my cheeks. "I just want to tell you that I'm sorry. I'm sorry that I can't help you. I'm so sorry that I can't make it better."

I spent the next several minutes there, alone with my son.

Sunday morning, the fifth day after he was born, Spencer got his first bath. They combed his hair, and put him in a little nightgown. They took off all the monitors and sensors, because now they were unnecessary. They removed all the tubes, except the breathing tube, and wrapped him in a blanket and handed him to us so that we could hold him in our arms for the first time. Our families came in, one by one, and said goodbye.

When all that could be done had been done, and all that could be said had been said, we told the staff in the NICU that we were ready. They removed the breathing tube, our symbol of hope for the past five days. I carried him into the family room, and closed the door.

Jennifer and I sat on the bed next to him.

"It'll be okay, Spencer. It'll all be over soon."

Jennifer held his hand and I kneeled over him. I wanted to be as close to him as I could get, so that he would know that he was not alone.

I looked into his little eyes and whispered, "It's okay. You can go now. I love you."

Not long after that, Spencer went from the arms of his earthly father, into the arms of his Heavenly Father.

Later that year, friends would say, "I don't know how you made it through. It must have been terrible."

Although I would never want to go through that kind of pain again, I knew at every juncture of the journey that we were all in God's hands. There was a sense of peace over Jennifer and me throughout the entire journey. Because of that peace, I always knew that everything was going to be okay.

It almost makes me feel guilty. Am I blocking the pain? Am I pretending this just did not happen? No, it did happen, and we accept it, and we credit God for that peace. God poured His grace over us throughout Spencer's life. We felt Him when we spent time together with Him in prayer. We felt His peace in the prayers of the people who love us at our church.

Now, when I think about Spencer, it is not so painful. He is still our son...our gift from God. We love him very much. To those without faith in God, it may seem that Spencer is no longer with us.

But we know that is not true. We know that he is up in heaven with God, watching over us every day.

And watching over his little brother, Levi, too.

Rejoice in the Lord always. I will say it again: Rejoice! Let your gentleness be evident to all. The Lord is near. Do not be anxious about anything, but in everything, by prayer and petition, with thanksgiving, present your requests to God. And the peace of God, which transcends all understanding, will guard your hearts and your minds in Christ Jesus."
Philippians 4:4-7

EIGHT
CHRIS

"Please don't be here for me," I prayed, as I saw the face of the principal, Sister Marie, in the window of my classroom door. Her salt and pepper hair hung in thick bangs and was cut severely just above her eyebrows. A sickening and familiar sense of horror rose in me and I held my breath. "Please," I prayed again. I hoped against hope that she was there to initiate a fire drill or to pass on some innocuous information to Mr. Dion, my 7th grade teacher. No, she had come for me. The tall, severe figure crooked her finger at me with that "shame on you" look, of which only nuns are capable.

As was often his practice, my father came to St. Claire's grade school and fabricated a reason to pull me out of class. He had plans for me and no school would keep him away from his own son. For him, two o'clock in the afternoon was the perfect time. My mom was still at work, and my sisters were still at the Catholic girls school they attended. He could take his time with me and enjoy himself. And, as always, there would be plenty of time for me to clean up the mess.

The dread I had for my father's plans that afternoon should have caused the shame from Sister Marie to pale in comparison. Yet for some reason, that I am still at a loss to explain, the shame I felt for not having notified her that I would be leaving class early actually rivaled the fear and pathetic resignation I felt for the events to come.

"Chris, time and time again you fail to mention your appointments and your poor father has to apologize for your forgetfulness. Next time you forget, it will mean detention for you," Sister Marie proclaimed with bitter authority. I walked past her to join my father. He gave me a twisted, all-knowing smile as he pushed me, in his not-so-gentle manner, toward the car.

"Scoot over right next to me," he said with a look of barely controlled excitement. He did not even have the patience to wait until we got home to dish out what he claimed, and I believed, I deserved. He made me sit right next to him on the big bench seat of his company car. Again, the embarrassment of being seen sitting so close to my father in a car did not escape me. Neither did his right hand. He could inflict unbearable pain with one hand while driving with the other.

We rounded the corner onto 14th street. Our house, a large, brown and white split level, was very typical of the 1970s. It appeared so nondescript and safe. Nobody could have suspected the ugly truths that were contained behind its walls.

CHRIS

My father released his grip on me. The pain of swinging my legs out to my right and across the car seat was almost worse. My body was no longer being numbed by a lack of blood flow, but it sent angry reminders to my brain of the previous attack. It was screaming about the pain that would soon be realized by every nerve ending.

"Get in the house," he growled. "We don't want to be late, do we?" His grin always launched my heart into my throat. As I passed my father in the doorway, I braced myself for his blows. With one hard smack, he sent me flying onto my face on the carpet.

"Get up!" he growled. My knuckles whitened as I clutched the carpet and pulled myself to my feet. I was 12 years old and extremely thin, but my body felt like it weighed 200 pounds as I stood and braced myself for another blow. "Into the kitchen," he ordered, some of the sick delight returning to his voice. The kitchen was his favorite place, second only to the bathtub for the ease of cleaning. I am not sure why he cared about that. I was the one who cleaned up the messes.

I peered at the counter top where he laid out his tools, and my heart jumped at what I saw. Surely, he could not really expect to use any of *these* implements!

My dad always planned our sessions ahead of time and with great pleasure. One implement was as horrible as the next, but always with a different twist. His favorite game was to have me choose. Today, my choices included a serrated kitchen knife, a rolling pin, and a very long, curved metal tube that came from our wading pool. My mind raced and at the last minute, I made my choice, hoping that somehow, the effect would be less severe than the other two.

My father's carefully planned and executed torture pushed me over the edge of what I could endure and I began to cry, "Please, please stop…I can't, I can't!"

My dad responded, "You're a filthy little boy and it's because of the devil in you that I have to do this to you. Do you think that this was my idea? It was yours. *You* told me that you wanted me to use this one."

Children believe everything that their parents tell them – outwardly when they are little, and inwardly as they grow older. I believed with all my heart that it was the evil little boy within me that made him do what he did. He made me apologize at the end of every session for what I was and take responsibility for everything that happened, including cleaning up the mess.

I learned to live in a fantasy world to escape my own. For years, I would close my eyes and imagine that the torture finally purged me of my evil and that my dad could joyfully announce to me that I was no longer filthy. I pictured him putting his arm around me or rumpling my hair like the fathers on TV did to their "clean" sons. At a certain age, the fantasy was too far out of reach. I changed it to visualizing someone else was my dad. I used to lie on my arm until it got numb, then I would pick it up with my other hand and run my own numb fingers through my hair. That way, it almost felt like someone else was doing it.

Later, I would try to figure out when it all began – how old was I? I know that it preceded my first communion at age five. I remember the priest saying, "Never bring shame to Christ by receiving communion with sins on your soul. Before receiving the Body of Christ, you will be required to make your first confession to have your sins absolved." I also remember kneeling in the confessional and reciting what I had learned: "Bless me Father for I have sinned, this is my first confession and these are my sins." I reeled off the usual transgressions of a five-year-old boy – I teased my sister, I lied, I lost my temper. "I have to tell him what I am," I thought, but I could not bring myself to say those words. When communion came, I closed my eyes and received the small wafer on my tongue saying, "Amen." It seemed I had shamed Christ and sealed my fate as an unredeemable, sinful little boy.

One afternoon, my father outdid even his own creativity. "Take off your clothes and lay face down on the floor," he barked. I obeyed, wondering why there were no tools evident and why he skipped the ritual of having me choose one. I was tempted, briefly, to believe that this time might be tolerable, but I knew better. One new session was more horrible then the last. "Now, lay still," he commanded, as I flattened myself against the cold linoleum.

I winced in disbelief as, one by one, my father drove straight pins through my skin and into the vinyl of the floor. I realized with horror that I had let out an audible gasp of pain. "Shut up, you filthy little scum!" he cried. When I thought that I could not stand the pain any longer, my father ordered me to stand up.

"I can't, Dad, I can't! Please don't make me!" Against my better judgment, I started crying and begging. His tone darkened as he hissed, "Get up, or we'll think of a fitting reward for your being such a wimp!"

I gritted my teeth and stood, feeling the pins pull through my flesh. "Now, clean up the mess," he said, almost gleefully, and walked away. On the floor, there was an outline of my body in pins, bits of flesh, and blood smears.

As I grew older, my father clearly resented the changes in my body. His frustration increased with each beating and he became less and less discrete. During one particularly violent session, my dad knocked me to the floor and came after me in his rage with his foot raised. He stomped down hard on my chest and I could hear bones cracking. "You disgust me!" he shouted, as he repeatedly kicked and stomped my chest and stomach, then threw me across the dining room table. Blood ran out of my mouth onto the tablecloth and I could barely see. I thought, "I am going to die this time – I'm going to die right here and go to hell!"

I could not move and could barely breathe. Then it occurred to me that my little sister would come home soon and find me this way. I loved her innocence. She actually looked up to me and tried to do everything I did. I could not bear the thought of her knowing what I was! Somehow, I found the strength to get up, clean up the mess and make it down to my bed.

The next morning, I could not make myself get out of bed. I heard my mom call the school. "I'm sorry," she said. "Chris won't be able to come to school for awhile. He has pneumonia." Later, this was the memory that forced me to accept that my mother knew. She knew it all.

I lay in bed for days with a broken collarbone and ribs. They were never set by a physician and remain asymmetrical to this day.

Once, when I was about 14, I sat in Sunday morning Mass and smelled the aroma of stale incense. I looked up at the crucifix and thought about Jesus. I thought about the hundreds of times that I begged Him to deliver me as my father tortured, beat, and raped me. My heart sank.

"There is no God," I thought. "If there is, then He must hate me. If He hates me, then I don't want anything to do with Him."

My plan was to survive my life until I could safely move out. The only dream that got me through was that someday I would become a functional adult and then, more than anything, I wanted a family and a small farm with animals – especially horses!

Two years later, I met a couple that lived in our neighborhood as I was walking my dog. First I met Rachel, who introduced herself to me and asked, "Would you baby-sit for us?" I eagerly agreed, always willing to make a few dollars and anxious for any excuse to be out of my house. I walked over later that evening and Rachel introduced me to her husband, James. This started a long friendship that God would use in a powerful way.

One evening, I was babysitting and saw a note that Rachel wrote for James; it read, "Nathan called with good news! Robert Woods decided to walk with the Lord!" I put the note down. Walk with the Lord? What on earth did that mean? I could not stop thinking about those words.

Rachel and James were so kind. I was drawn to them and wanted to be with them whenever I could. I used to walk my dog past their house and if they were not home, I would hide around the corner just outside of view. Whenever I saw headlights coming down the street, I would casually start walking. Most of the time, it was someone else. Eventually, they would return and would marvel at how amazing it was that God delivered me to their driveway just when they were coming home.

I lied to my parents and started attending church with Rachel and James. I also went to the youth group there. There was so much love in the people at that church – even from the kids my age. I wanted that same love in my heart. Although I could not put it into words, there was something else there that I desperately wanted.

CHRIS

After service once, James knelt next to me. "Chris," he said. "Have you ever accepted Jesus as your Savior?" I shook my head. "I know you know all about Him, and that you do good things," he said, "but there is another step. You need to acknowledge your sins and ask Him into your heart. He is the *only* way to eternal life. If you ask Him to come, He will live in you and never leave you." James walked me through the prayer, and when I repeated "amen" after him, I opened my eyes to see him smiling at me. As I drove home, I realized the miracle that Jesus now lived in me – in my heart! I was so over-come with joy. I wanted everyone to know what God had done for me, and that they could have the joy and peace of Jesus in their hearts, too.

Meanwhile, the beatings from my dad continued and my health declined. It was not unusual for me to pass out cold at the dinner table. I even passed out one night as I walked home with some friends after youth group. I was six feet tall and weighed about 120 pounds. The episodes with my father gave way to rages in him that often resulted in my wearing very visible bruises, black eyes and split lips. One day, a friend insisted that I get out of my parent's house. He advised me, "Go home, apologize for everything you have ever done to offend your dad, and insist that you have to move out of his home. Then call me, and I'll come get you. There are plenty of families you can live with."

I did not have the courage to have this conversation with my dad, but I did sit down with my mom that night. "I can't take Dad's beatings anymore, Mom. I have to move out," I told her cautiously.

"Please don't leave," she said softly. "If you do, he will only take it out on your younger sister." I could not stand the thought of passing my role on to her. My heart was overwhelmed with the responsibility of it all. I looked at her face and suddenly her expression changed. "No! You won't be going – he will! Tomorrow I want you to go away with some friends for the day. He will be gone before you return!"

The next day I was happier than I had ever been. My mom was on my side. She promised not to tell my dad about our conversation and that she would have him removed. I was coming home to a safe family!

The minute I returned, I knew that everything had gone wrong. My father stood in the stairwell. The look in his face told me that his fury had reached new heights. Mom had told him everything. He commanded me into his bedroom. Quietly poised on the edge of the bed, my mother was in tears. Her betrayal was as thick as the Bible my dad held in his hand. "Put your hand on this Bible and swear, in front of me, your mother, and God, that I have never laid a hand on you," he said, with every confidence that I would obey. He had no reason to doubt that I would do just as he said. Despite my fear that I would lose God by lying, I indeed put my hand on the Bible. "No, you have never hurt me," I said. My mother was excused

CHRIS

and my father beat and raped me without mercy. I noticed that the statue of Mary on his dresser seemed to look down on me with sadness as he finished and left me on the wooden floor beneath her gaze.

I called my friend and continued the lie. I told him that my father said he would never beat me again and that our family would get counseling. So I avoided my Christian friends when my body showed evidence of his violence.

Finally, when I was 17 years old, I knew it was time to break away and move out. James and Rachel had moved to the country and invited me to go live with them. At last I gathered the courage to discuss it with my mother.

"Mom, I have not been Catholic for a couple of years and I really need to get away from here. I will always love you. I hope you understand." My mom looked worn out and sad. She said nothing as she turned and walked away.

After I moved in, James and Rachel noticed how incredibly ill I was. Besides being painfully thin, I often woke up bleeding on my pillow as I slept. Occasionally, I passed out without warning. The doctor told me I had very advanced bleeding ulcers.

One day, James' parents invited me over for dinner. I was a little uncomfortable because it was just the three of us and it was my first time there. Nevertheless, they welcomed me and were full of love, just like their son. After the meal, James' dad said, "Now it is time to pray for you." He and his wife were strong in their faith, but many other people had already prayed for me. Why would this time be any different?

When they were done, they looked very jubilant and said, "You are healed." They even called James and Rachel as soon as I left. "We prayed for him," they said, "and he was healed, praise the Lord!" They read Bible verses to me about Jesus walking and visiting towns and healing people. I cherished the parts that read, "And all were healed." When I went home that night, Jesus spoke to my heart and I knew in my spirit that I was healed. For the first time, I actually believed it. At my next scheduled doctor's appointment, I learned the good news: all the ulcers were gone. Only scar tissue remained.

Over the years, God has completely changed my life. Statistically, I should not be a functioning adult, but people who know me now would never even suppose that I had this background at all. Jesus introduced me to the one true Father, who will never fail me and whose heart ached with mine at every pain inflicted on me. I have had to learn to trust people, especially other men, and I also needed to change the pattern of assuming that I am despised. Jesus loves me just as I am. He suffered so much more on the cross than I did at home, just so I could be His.

After the birth of my second child, there was a time where I could barely sleep for fear of the chronic nightmares about my childhood. It was so bad that I could think of very little else during the day. I was exhausted and difficult to be around. A Christian brother walked through those memories with me and reviewed every ugly detail, applying God's grace and acceptance. I would close my eyes and whisper some of the details to him; I was so ashamed of what happened to me. When I opened my eyes, I expected to see a look of shock, disgust or, at the very least, a resolve never to ask me again; but I saw only tears of compassion. They were like the tears that Jesus shed for me. It was the beginning of God's complete healing. Today, those memories have no sting, no power over me!

God gave me an exceptionally smart and beautiful wife and incredible children. We live in a big house, on a farm, with horses, my dream come true. When I realize that God entrusted me with the gift of my wife, and when I look at my kids and know that God loves me even more than I love them, I do not know how I could be sad about anything in the past. I cannot draw on the love of my earthly father to understand the love of God, but I have seen our Heavenly Father's love toward me through Christ-like friends and through my family. Best of all, He has taught me what a true father's heart is through the love he gave me for my own precious children.

I do not consider myself a victim of anything, and I do not tend to use the term "survivor." I am a conqueror, through Christ. He won the battle before it was even waged on me. 1 Corinthians 1:3 says: "Blessed be the God of all comfort, who comforts those in their afflictions so that they may be able to comfort others with that comfort that God has given them." I pray that when I comfort others in their struggles, it is not me, but Christ that puts His arm around them, Christ that chooses my words, and Christ's heart that is represented.

Ilive with physical reminders of my past. My collarbone is still pointed the wrong way; my ribs are still asymmetrical, yet God has completely healed me. Jesus was raised from the dead, though He still had scars on His hands and side. Thomas needed to touch those scars so he could believe Jesus was really alive. Would I rather my scars not exist? Not really. They remind me of God's faithfulness. He made me an overcomer of seemingly impossible circumstances and gave me all the desires of my heart. Maybe someday, others will touch my scars and believe!

NINE
JAMIE HARRIS

"YOU KILLED HIM! YOU KILLED HIM!" These were the first words I heard when I picked up the phone early that morning 15 years ago.

"What? Who is this? What are you talking about?" I whispered back into the receiver.

"Kenny. You killed my nephew, Kenny!" Then the phone line went dead.

Instantly, my heart started racing. Confused, home alone, and without a license, I called my mom's fiancé. It was all I could do to steady my fingers and dial his number.

"Larry! Can you come get me? I...I...I'm so scared...I don't know...I think he's...I...I..." I spoke incoherently, but Larry heard the distress and urgency in my voice and came over immediately.

He picked me up and took me back to his house. Larry's training as a firefighter gave him the words of assurance I needed to hear at that moment. "Calm down, honey. Let's not jump to any conclusions. I'm sure everything is going to be all right." He turned up his emergency dispatch scanner to see if there was any news. It did not take long to hear that an ambulance had been sent.

"Please let him be alive, please let him be alive," I said out loud. I reasoned that if an ambulance was called, Kenny was still alive.

The phone rang.

"Hello," Larry answered. "Yes, uh huh, uh huh. Okay, thank you." It was the fire station. They had promised to call him back as soon as they knew anything. I looked in his eyes and I knew.

"He's dead isn't he?" I asked, already knowing the answer.

"Yes, he is." Larry said. "I'm so sorry, Jamie."

Kenny was dead and I was being blamed. My mind reeled with the events of the last two days. I had gone to the Friday night high school dance with my girlfriends. Kenny and I were in another fight; one of many in our on-again-off-again relationship, and some other guy gave me a ride home. Just a simple ride home, but I guess that was too much for Kenny. He called me up Saturday and yelled, "Who gave you a ride home? Is he your new boyfriend? What did you do with him?" he bellowed.

"I didn't do anything with him! He just gave me a ride home! I'm so tired of our roller coaster relationship. I can't take it anymore! I think it's time we break up!" I fired back at him. "And flowers and poems won't win me back this time." I added that more to convince myself than Kenny.

"Fine. But just know that I am going to kill myself today. Oh, and don't flatter yourself...I would never commit suicide over *you*," he emphasized. I never believed that he would kill himself. He had cried wolf too many times for his threats to bear any weight. However, I found myself a day later at the cold, busy police station reading a beautiful goodbye letter Kenny had written to me.

When we went to the funeral a few days later, Kenny's popularity was evident. The memorial service was filled with hundreds of people who came to say goodbye to this boy. I looked for a warm, familiar face but the seniors from his class and the sophomores from mine seemed uncomfortable around me. The stained glass windows and beautiful flowers were a stark contrast to the dark colors and heavy winter coats that filled the sanctuary. I sat on the pew next to my mother and Larry and cried for Kenny. We all did.

"If Kenny could be anywhere right now, he'd be on the top of a mountain with his snowboard on fresh powder, mastering the half pipe," one friend said into the microphone. Someone started to chuckle to confirm this statement, but sounded unsure if happiness was allowed at a funeral.

The funeral director read the letter I had written to Kenny next. It was filled with my most tender feelings and memories and included one of the many poems Kenny had written to me. What an incredibly talented and loving person he was. "What a loss," I thought, "that someone with that much talent and creativity would no longer write, or snowboard, or build anything ever again."

After the service, my mom and Larry helped me with my coat and practically carried me out to the car. When they opened the double doors leading outside, I gasped. We stepped out into the brisk, fresh air to find snow falling all around. It glistened in the trees and put an ever so appropriate hush to the noisy world. "Thank you, God, for sending snow on this February day...a day to remember Kenny and his love for the snow," I prayed quietly.

I heard a faint knock outside my bedroom door later that evening. "Come in," I said. It was my mother.

"Do you want to talk?" she asked, in that loving way mothers have.

We talked about the day I met Kenny up at The Cliffs swimming hole and the fun vacations he took with us. We continued talking into the early hours of the morning.

"Mom, will you sleep with me tonight?" I asked.

She let out an obvious sigh of relief and said, "Of course, honey." I know that she was worried that I might be thinking about taking my own life. She was such a steadfast love in my life. I drifted off to sleep in the comfort of my mother's arms every night for the next two months.

JAMIE HARRIS

Several days later I barely scraped myself together and entered dance practice at 6 a.m. My teammates, not knowing what to say and being warned not to talk about it and make me cry, all did exactly that.

"Oh, Jamie, are you okay?" one girl asked. "I'm here for you, Jamie," another girl said. We sat there on the gym floor in a tangled mess of hugs and tears for several minutes.

Sitting in my classroom was a different story. I could feel the gaze of the other students as they stared at the girl whose boyfriend just committed suicide. "Is someone talking to me?" I thought, and turned to look, but was met with averted eyes and abrupt endings to conversations. As I walked to my locker one afternoon, I could see in the distance that something looked different. Something felt wrong about the hallway. With each step I took, I sensed something horrible. As I neared my locker, I heard giggling and looked around to see people scattering out of sight. "Oh my gosh!" I said under my breath. "Who would do this?" There on my locker was a perfect noose attached to the air vent. Tears welled as I struggled to remove this sick joke. The corners of my mouth quivered and a lump formed in my throat as I held back my true emotions. Some time later, I had the same dread as I walked out to my car. Having just received my license, I was happy to be on the road. But something was not right. I could see something in the distance. Is that black oil? I stood there in shock as I read the word "MURDERER" smeared on the side of my car.

I do not blame anyone for his or her accusations. I know they are just hurt and taking it out on me. I will forgive them. I reminded myself of this every single day, but I vowed never to date again.

"I won't take no for an answer," a cute boy said, smiling his sly grin at me.

"Okay, see you Friday night," I said, finally giving in to both this persistent suitor as well as breaking my vow. That proved to be a mistake I would soon regret.

A couple of months later I shouted, "Let me go! You're hurting me!" He had me forcibly by my arm as we yelled at each other. "I'm tired of all this fighting and I just want our relationship over! Aren't you sick of fighting too?" I was barely able to keep from screaming as he pulled me around. My temperature rose as I struggled with my boyfriend and the cold air felt good against my body.

"You want to break up with me?" he shouted. "Huh? Do ya? Go ahead. Do it. I'll commit suicide. That's right. Then you'll have *two* deaths on your conscience," he mocked.

"I don't care. I am so emotionally dead right now, that if you did, I wouldn't care." I said. And I really didn't. Then I heard a noise that I could not identify, yet it was loud and in my head. Opening my eyes I saw the world sideways, felt hard pavement under my cheek, and realized the sound was my head being slammed against the garage door. His suicide threat was just that; a threat, but that ending to our relationship left me feeling equally unsettled.

When I went off to college in Portland, I felt alone. I was afraid of being by myself and I did not know anyone. I called my mom. "I'm scared," I cried. "I'm a little lonely and this is such a big city."

Mom was always willing to talk day or night. "I'll be right there, honey," was always her reply. She often drove the two hours to stay with me in my tiny college apartment and helped me get adjusted.

Soon friendships developed and I settled in. Several different boyfriends allowed me to have fun partying in frat houses without the agonizing commitment of a long-term relationship. Breaking up before we fell in love was easier than risking a potential suicide, but having so many boyfriends was emotionally draining me.

During my first year, as I lay in bed trying to sleep, I was bothered by a peculiar sound and forced myself awake. I found my boyfriend standing over me. "What are you doing here? What are you *doing*?" I asked. Rubbing the sleep out of my eyes and adjusting to the light, I realized he was tearing up a dozen roses he was going to give me. The angry look in his eyes and the silence that prevailed let me know, all too well, that the single rose from someone else there on my dresser infuriated him.

"Hey, please don't be upset," I begged.

"You expect me not to be upset when I bring you a dozen flowers only to find some other *dude* has brought you one?" he shrieked.

My response was simple and unexpected. "I'm pregnant and it's yours."

A few days later, sitting in his dad's office, I read the doctorate degrees and specialized awards hanging on the wall. My thoughts were interrupted when someone spoke.

"Are you sure this is what you want?" his dad asked.

"Yes, this is my decision." I said, feebly.

He sighed with disappointment but, being a professional, he arranged and paid for the whole cost of the abortion.

The clock read 3:48. Was that a.m. or p.m.? I wondered. I did not flinch when the telephone rang. I was tired of the answering machine messages. Jamie, your assignment is overdue. Jamie, weren't you going to come over today? Jamie, it's me, your friend, call me. Jamie, it's your mom, call me. Jamie, WHERE ARE YOU?

I stumbled to the bathroom and looked at myself in the mirror. Seven days of tears staining my face, seven days in the same t-shirt and sweats, seven days with little or no food revealed my agony. The bathroom scale exposed a number I was shocked to see, but how *could* I eat? How could I do anything after what I had done? I went back to bed and thoughts of summer camp, when I was younger, flooded my head. Yes, I gave my life to Jesus that night when the pastor was leading us in prayer. "Do you remember that, God?" I asked. "I'm sorry. I'm sorry I had an abortion. I'm sorry I even had sex to begin with!" I lay there with my face buried in my pillow crying for the bad choices I had made. "God, will you forgive me? I'm so sorry!" I sat up and the room grew a little warmer. I felt a love in my soul. "Thank you, God, for being here," I finished praying.

Just before graduation, I made another vow: no more boyfriends! The two-year relationship I had just ended was just as emotionally exhausting as the relationships I had for only a few months. "No, Sean," I said. "I don't want a boyfriend." I tried to turn him down gently; he was not aware of the tumultuous, roller coaster life I had with past relationships.

"So, when can I call you next?" was his response. His romantic persistence wore me down and eventually I agreed. He was so different from anyone I had dated and our relationship was so unlike any I had ever had. Sean never raised his voice. He was so steady and even. Even his mother seemed happy we were together.

"Oh, honey, I hope my son marries someone like you," she gushed. "You're just the kind of woman he needs." I sat on her soft, blue sofa thumbing through baby photos of my new boyfriend. Finally, what a perfect situation I was in.

The waves of the Oregon coast crashed in the distance as I buried my feet in the sand. Sean and I had only been together for six months and I was already allowing myself to fall in love with him. And, I knew he felt the same for me. Our love was just like the ocean – steady, strong, and constant. The wind was slight and breezy, but the sun beating down warmed my face. I whispered a silent prayer of thanks to God for bringing me this man. As I looked over at Sean, he seemed anxious. His eyes were darting and he kept clearing his throat. We got up to walk toward the water. "Why does he keep turning around?" I wondered. Then, when the unusually crowded shoreline began to clear of people, Sean stopped in his tracks. Grabbing both my hands and turning me toward him, I looked up at his face only to see that his whole body was lowering to one knee. I gasped and my eyes grew twice as big. This is the moment every little girl, every teenager, and every young lady awaits. As the sun was setting, it spread a purple hue across the sky. Everything was perfect! We were alone on the beach as Sean said, "Jamie, I love you. Will you marry me?"

I was not feeling well that morning and ran to the bathroom to throw up, again. "Oh no," I thought, "am I really?" Sean and I sat on the edge of the tub, not talking. I twisted my fingers and he sat still. Those three minutes seemed like three hours. We held our breath as we both looked at the pregnancy test. Two lines. Two lines! "Oh Sean, I'm pregnant. The wedding is in three months!" I exclaimed. "What are we going to do?"

We weighed the options. We talked ourselves in and out of

it a hundred different ways. Finally, we made our decision.

"I've done it before."

"No one will know."

"We're not ready to be parents."

"Your mother would freak out!"

"Insurance will pay for the whole thing."

"It's legal."

We hit every red light on the way to the clinic. My fiancé drove with the same, steady calm of his personality, but the tears in his eyes betrayed his outward appearance. Walking up the stairs to the foyer, I tried to remember if this building looked anything like the previous one, when I had done this before. Nothing came to the forefront of my memory. We sat in the waiting room amongst the outdated hunting and housekeeping magazines, the other nervous patients, and the hushed voices of the personnel. I looked at Sean just as he was looking at me. The same question blurted from our lips, "Are we doing the right thing?" Before we could answer, my name was called.

The scenic paintings were meant to calm us, as well as the flowers, but Sean and I were tense with our decision. The preparatory questions and paperwork seemed to drag on forever. "Hurry up," I thought. "Let's just get it over with."

I looked up at the cracks in the ceiling and tried not to feel so exposed as the doctor turned on the machine. Sean's comforting hand squeezed mine, he knelt down toward my face and we let our tears stream together as the horrible sound of the vacuum defined the procedure.

"Pull over, Sean, I'm going to puke again," I said. Sean eased to the side of the road and waited patiently for me to finish. This was the second time he had to pull over so my body could purge the anguish I felt as we drove home that evening. The emergency blinkers fooled passing drivers into thinking perhaps we had car problems. Every automobile that drove by seemed to carry happy people. How could the world go on as if nothing had happened? Didn't they know what I had just done? My own thoughts were now betraying my decision. Could I have made a mistake?

A single question kept racing around my mind. I didn't want to ask it because I was afraid of the answer but, finally, I did. "Sean, will God forgive us? Will He forgive *me*?"

Sean never responded. I guess he did not know the answer. We agreed to forget about it. "Let's just never talk about it or think about it. Deal?"

"Deal." This was our commitment to each other. I tried really hard to stick to it, but even reading a book or watching television proved to be hard. Something always crept in to remind me.

Our wedding was perfect and our trip to Mexico was wonderful. It was so comforting to live with my best friend;

still, the first year was rough, often reeling on the brink of disaster. We decided to try to have a baby, but month after month, I never got pregnant.

"This is our payback for the abortion! We deserve this, don't we Sean?" I asked. "It's been two and a half years and we can't get pregnant. Tell me this isn't our punishment." I blamed him and myself.

When I finally did get pregnant, multiple complications and even the cesarean section added to my self-condemnation. This was my penance.

"Jamie, let's just keep looking. One of these churches has got to be able to help us find an answer from God," my husband reasoned. We felt so lost and sinful and we were fighting all the time. Somehow, we knew God was the answer to help save our marriage.

The several different churches we tried all had nice people, but not one of them seemed to be able to connect with us. We always felt alone in the middle of a huge congregation. The Mormon classes were time-consuming and, in the end, left us with just as many questions as we had at the beginning of our search.

"A guy I work with, Cliff Brady, goes to Living Hope Fellowship. He keeps telling me about this group he gets together with called The Young Marrieds. Maybe we should check it out," I suggested.

Sean stared at me from across the room and replied, "What

have we got to lose?"

I squeezed Sean's hand as we walked into the house. Would people be friendly? Judgmental? I had so many questions. Besides, this was Jess Strickland's house, the head Pastor! We sat on dining room chairs that lined the living room. There was the stuffy smell of socked feet, people crammed in everywhere, and iced coffee. I leaned over to Sean and whispered, "They all keep talking about God as if they really know Him. They all pray to Him."

"Yeah," he replied. "I noticed that, too."

Cliff's wife, Tiffany, reached out and put her hand on my leg. I looked around and most of the heads were bowed as someone led out in prayer. Some people had their heads raised toward the heavens. With Tiffany's hand on my leg, I could feel Jesus' love pour out of her and into me. A warm sensation came over me again; the same loving feeling I had when I accepted Jesus back at summer camp; the same love I felt when I lay in my college bed for a week straight; the same love I felt when I asked God to forgive me for my first abortion. Jesus was in this very room, this very moment and I could feel Him!

The darkness hid our faces as we walked out that night, but the exuberance Sean and I both felt from that wonderful evening spent with the Young Marrieds' group lit us up from the inside out. As we slid into the car and shut the doors, we looked at each other and agreed we were definitely going back to that group! The connection to each other, the way everyone just talked to and about God was exactly what we were looking for. Already a void was being filled in our lives. The flame that was ignited in our hearts during our own talks with God so many years ago had been breathed on that night, and it started to grow.

The same feeling of love and acceptance we received at Young Marrieds was equally shared at church as Sean and I started regularly attending. We could feel in our lives that it was not just the love from the people, but also the love of God *through* them towards us. Sean and I fully committed our lives to God a short time later. Heart-to-heart talking every night in our house was now a sought after event. Our bickering and arguing was replaced with meaningful conversation, prayer, confession, and love for each other. Our love had been made new, fresh and more concrete because we made Jesus the center of our marriage.

One Sunday I waited quietly, with great anticipation alongside my husband. The congregation outside was singing and then the music died down. I was first. I stepped down the steep, tiny stairs into the lukewarm water of the baptismal tank. Pastor Daren Lindley and Cliff Brady were there with me ready to guide me in this act of faith. All the Young Marrieds couples surrounded the tank as first I, then Sean was baptized. The waters of baptism released me of the sins and self-loathing I had heaped upon myself.

A year later, I had the same anxiety as I stood before the

congregation again. Looking out, I could tell that attendance was doubled this Easter Sunday. The lighting changed so that it made it hard for me to see past the first few rows. My palms were sweaty and my hands shaky, but I knew in my heart this was something I wanted to tell everyone. My voice trembled only a little as I stood in front of what seemed like the whole world and read my life story. The shame of my choices was released entirely that morning as I told everyone how God changed my heart in so many ways.

My outlook on life has changed because of my commitment to God. Holidays have real, true meaning for my family and me. I now believe God gives us children so we will understand how much He loves us! The guilt and shame that once weighed me down has been lifted. I have been blessed many times over since believing in God and have received the gift of love and acceptance from Him. I now have one daughter and she is the biggest blessing by far.

My faith in God is unwavering and steadfast. There is an ongoing relationship that is strengthened every day by my praying and reading the Bible. Living with God in my heart is a peaceful, joyful, life-changing experience. I have no doubt He is with me every day. I struggle with things in life as everyone does, but now I have God to guide me and comfort me. I know He will continue to shape me into the person He wants me to be, until my last day on earth. A verse I rely on quite often is Proverbs 3:5-6: "Trust in the Lord with all your heart and lean not on your own understanding; in all ways acknowledge Him and He will make your path straight."

TEN
JULIE PENN

Sitting in the cafeteria, my best friend leaned over and whispered, "Well, did you do it?" She had a huge smile on her face as she read the expression on mine. I could not hide the fact that I did have sex, for the very first time, the night before.

"Another one bites the dust," she said. This phrase was to welcome me into a club of girls who had lost their virginity that year. I felt the sting of those words. I had done something I really was not proud of and I knew there was no going back.

Trying to remain a virgin had not been easy. I attended a big, public high school where an acceptance of sex between boyfriends and girlfriends had permeated our campus. I grew up in a Christian home and knew this kind of relationship would not be best for me, but I was unsure about the choices I wanted to make in my life. Instead, I went along with whatever seemed fun at the time. In adolescence, it was much easier to agree with the prevailing peer opinion. When the popular classmates pronounced something "cool," it inevitably became cool.

Because I had not made well-thought-out decisions for myself, I simply let someone else make the choice for me. In this case, I gave away my virginity to another's temporary desire. It was the beginning of more hurt than I could have known.

My next few boyfriends did not pressure me into having sex, though the relationships never lasted very long. When I turned 18, I began dating David and was ready to put the past behind me and live a good, clean, Christian life. At 22, David was handsome, funny, and friendly to everyone. He seemed to be the perfect boyfriend for me. We had met at work and loved to spend our break time talking about anything and everything. We frequently went out after work just so we could talk some more.

"So, are you a virgin?" David asked me.

"Yes," I lied. I wanted David to have a good impression of me. I tried to forget, or perhaps ignore the person I was in high school and convince David that I was the "perfect" Christian girl he seemed to want. "I *can* be that girl," I thought, and planned never to talk about my high school relationship.

During high school, I was not motivated to accomplish high-set goals, and casually breezed by classes with average grades. I was more interested in hanging out with my boyfriend than taking the SATs. Still, I assumed that after high school I would go to college, learn about that new phase of life, and buckle down to study when it really counted.

"We are sorry to inform you that we are unable to admit you to our university," the letter began. It was from Oregon State University, where all my girlfriends were going that fall. Shocked, I felt the first downward nudge of my self-esteem.

I got a job at a pizza restaurant and began attending Portland State part-time. Nevertheless, each time I talked to my friends at OSU it only reminded me that I was not smart enough to get in, and when I drove down and spent the weekend visiting my friends on campus, I had to wipe away furious tears on the trip home.

"God, why can't I be there? I want to live that life! I want to be with my friends and have fun at those parties! I want to study on that huge green lawn in the sunshine, and be a part of that college scene! Why won't you let me? Am I stupid? Did you make me with less intelligence than them? I know you didn't make me stupid, but I feel that way. Why did it all happen like this?"

I started putting myself down, making self-degrading comments about my intelligence: "That is something *I'll* never be able to understand." I would avoid talking about difficult topics such as politics or technology, believing they were over my head. To compound this, I got a raise at the pizza place because the manager said he thought I was pretty. "I guess I'm just not smart, but at least I'm pretty," I deduced.

A few months later, David's and my relationship became

serious. David tried to make sure I was really the person with whom he wanted to spend his life. There were a few qualities he wanted in a spouse that it seemed I did not possess – mainly, an ability to cook. Boxed food and take-out dinners should not be the continual sustenance for a family. In addition, David is very smart. Sometimes, just being around him can make you feel like you are a step behind in the conversation. It was not that he believed I was dumb. He thought that maybe he should marry someone who had pursued a more academic life, someone with whom he could enjoy intellectual discussions. I was devastated when he ended our relationship. I was already susceptible to negative thoughts about my intellect, so when he told me his reasons, the wounds to my self-worth reopened. I felt as if I was losing control over my own life. I did not get to go to the college I wanted; now, I do not get to keep the man I wanted. How can I gain control?

David and I continued our friendship and I continued my pursuit to get what I wanted. Not long afterwards, he came to a realization.

"Julie, it is *you* that I love, not the things you can or cannot do." He apologized for ending our relationship and soon after, we became engaged. More and more I considered that my only talents were in my looks. I questioned if David came back to me because he loved me, or because I continued flirting with him in attempt to win back his heart.

Enjoying the power of manipulation and seduction, I persuaded David into going too far physically before marriage. Sitting on the sofa during our premarital counseling, we squeezed each other's hand when we heard the counselor say, "Well, the next subject we should talk about is intimacy."

"Yeah, well, we're both virgins," I said. This rolled off my tongue with ease and David did not say anything to contradict me. We had prearranged to deny our sin if the topic of sex was brought up. It seemed that lying was becoming a habit with me. An added feeling to my low self-esteem was guilt.

We were finally married and I thought it would be over.

"I'm free now. I have a clean slate," I tried to convince myself. I reasoned that I entered a new phase of my life as a married woman that would allow me to forget about my past sins. Yet I had not confessed, nor been forgiven, so the sinful habits still gripped me. No, I could not forget anything. Guilt started taking over my every emotion.

I flirted frequently on my new job at Intel. Having more male friends than female was a part of my identity at that point. At the same time, David sometimes teased me about my cooking, or intellect – nothing meant to be harmful – but each time, it stung. I felt I had to prove that I was worthy of being his wife.

Early in our marriage, we decided that I should quit college so we could save the money. After all, it was likely I would stay home if we had children, so there was no need for a degree. For years, regret about that decision plagued me. When we changed our minds about having kids at all, I realized a degree could have helped me get more raises and promotions. I resented losing the chance to prove that I had what it took to complete a degree. Still, the decision had been made and it was not the time to change course. I threw myself into my job and achieved what I could. Soon I had a great position, gained some needed confidence, and began to believe that I might be smarter than I had previously thought.

One day, at the end of a seminar, one of the participants with whom I had been flirting all week approached me. More than once I had gone out for a drink with these older, richer, businessmen. It was a thrilling sensation to have so much control over these situations. Men enjoyed being around me, a feeling I did not get from my husband. I ignored the nagging voice in my head telling me it was wrong. I did not know how to stop what I had started and gave in to a few physical offers. It was not about the sex; enjoying the power of manipulation was my goal at a time in my life when I felt I could not control anything else.

I stopped talking to God. How could I talk to Him – the Creator of my life and of the whole world – when He knew what I had done? I did not know what to pray about, for it was ludicrous to ask for blessings or protection when I continued in my sin every day. I stopped reading my Bible – too convicting. I knew I could not hide from God, but I was doing everything I could to stay away from Him. I was so ashamed to call myself a Christian, yet to lead such a fraudulent lifestyle. Spending Sunday morning at church with David became increasingly unbearable. I did not like the guilt and asked myself, "Who do you think you are?"

"A liar," was the answer that quickly came back to me.

I decided to get advice. The professional counselor whom I contacted through my insurance encouraged me that David was the problem. "David has given you poor self-esteem. He pushed you into this behavior." I knew it was not true. I was responsible for my actions. A few misspoken comments, as happen in every marriage, are not cause for infidelity. In reality, I knew that I was smart, but I had simply given in to self-pity for too long.

A couple of years went by and though I had not accepted any more physical offers, I became sick from guilt and shame. I had been with other men and was hiding this from my spouse, the one I loved deeply. What if he found out? He would not believe me if I told him I loved him and that I was sorry. Why would he believe that? No, he would divorce me.

There was no sure route I could take in my life, so I opted for the one that seemed to bring the least amount of agony to my husband. I resigned myself to hiding my sin forever. I told myself that I could manage to live with guilt and shame if that meant not telling anyone of my affairs. Of course, sin makes us miserable and I spiraled downward. I could not talk to David, God, or anyone close to me. I knew that if I tried to talk to anyone about the agony I was feeling, the truth would be revealed and my husband would find out. I just could not bear that. Emotionally, I sank lower and lower into darkness. Our marriage grew distant and gray.

Many sleepless nights I lay awake agonizing over my poor choices. My mind reeled with questions and thoughts about my life. "Maybe I didn't love David and that's why I cheated on him! No, I *do* love him, I do! Why did I do that? I can't tell him anything…he would be so hurt. I don't even care anymore if he left me; I just can't inflict that much emotional pain on him. It would be better if I were gone. I'll just leave. I'll get in my car and start over in a new town. No, that wouldn't make sense to anyone. I wish I were dead," I thought to myself.

These thoughts ran through my mind every single night as I lay next to my husband. I even thought of different suicide notes I could write or how to make a fatal car crash look like an accident. Death was more appealing than facing the truth with my husband or God. Sometimes, I would look at the Bible on my shelf and would immediately have to turn away. Or I would utter the beginning of a prayer, "Dear God," but would stop and think of something else. For every time I allowed God into my thoughts, I was always met with the same feeling of a need to confess. But that was not the path I chose to live my life, so I ignored those feelings. My heart was so heavy with guilt and shame that I became depressed and lonely. Between the stress and the fact that I no longer had a relationship with God, my life and marriage were miserable.

"Why are we fighting all the time?" David asked.

"I don't know. Why are you always so grumpy?" I snapped back.

"I'm grumpy because you're always mad at me."

"Well, maybe I'm mad because you're constantly grumpy!"

It was always the same after too many fights about nothing: I would cry myself to sleep and David would lay beside me angry. More than once we convinced ourselves that we had nothing in common. David played tennis and I snow-skied; he read science fiction, I read novels; he liked computers, I liked shopping.

"Why did we get married?" was the common question in our household.

"I want a divorce," I finally said. I did not really want one, but I wanted to free my husband of an unworthy wife. It was unfair for him to be married to someone so unfaithful.

We filed for divorce and I moved back to my parents' home. David knew nothing of why this was happening. He chocked it up to incompatibility, but he still loved me. It was a very amicable separation; he offered to take on all the debt, and pay for everything. David was so incredibly caring. Even during the process of our divorce, he sent me flowers.

"The poor guy. He doesn't even know why I've left him. This is so unfair to him," I would say to myself, but I still could not face telling him the truth. I wanted some other way around this, but I knew all the blame rested on me. It ate at my conscience.

Having unconfessed sin in my life was miserable. I never wanted to cheat. I never wanted to lie and hide. I never wanted to go through a divorce. I did not care about the power of seduction anymore. I was sick of it all. My life was so unbalanced; it was almost unrecognizable even to me. Going to work, going to church, having dinner with my parents, talking with David...these everyday things were unbearable because of the guilt.

"What started the path that got me to a place of unhappiness and shame?" I wondered. "Was it losing my virginity in high school? Was it not being accepted to a big college? Was it the affairs? Was it hiding so much from my husband?" I was so confused and reached a point where something had to change.

In desperation, I went to a dear friend. It was the pastor who had baptized me, performed my wedding, and someone I knew I could trust. He was in the middle of moving offices so he was temporarily set up in a Sunday school room, complete with pictures of Jesus with children and memory verses taped to the wall in bright colors. It was awkward to come to him with such a heavy topic while sitting among toys and signs of happiness and love.

"Pastor Wayne, I have so much to say," I started, breathing a heavy sigh that preceded the telling of my ugly life.

"Go ahead," he said, kindly and patiently.

"I'm keeping a secret from my husband. If I tell him, he will be so hurt and feel so betrayed that I just can't bear to tell him. But if I don't tell him, the lie will eat me alive. I should be the better person and take the pain rather than transferring it to my husband, right? I don't know what to do. Nothing seems right," I said.

Pastor Wayne was very concerned but in a loving way urged me to continue.

"I cheated on my husband," I said, almost whispering. I told him everything that was on my heart; all the sin along with the guilt I had been carrying. I also told him about the feelings I had been getting every time I thought about God; the feeling that God wanted me to do something I did not want to do.

After leaning forward with his elbows on his knees, Pastor Wayne reclined and took a deep breath. A compassionate look swept over his face and he said, "Julie, the truth will set you free." Tears fell like rain as I dropped my head into my hands and came to the end of myself. It was as if God Himself spoke straight into my soul and gave me the answer for everything. I instantly understood that if I would confess, telling the truth to both David and God, I would be *free* from this sin and heavy guilt. The Sunday school room now seemed very appropriate for me to be in, as I felt like a child returning to the arms of her father; only I was returning to the arms of my Heavenly Father.

I drove to my house and cautiously knocked on the door. David welcomed me in. "I have something to tell you." I said softly. We went to the living room. He stood at the fireplace while I sat on the couch, disconsolate and scared. He could tell that whatever I had to say was going to be bad news.

"You slept with somebody else," he guessed.

"Yes." I paused while tears instantly came to David's eyes.

"But it gets worse," I said.

"You slept with your boyfriend in high school, didn't you?" There was now audible pain in his voice.

"Yes."

With both of us crying, David walked over to the couch, sat down, and put his arms around me.

"Julie, I forgive you. I love you so much. I forgive you," he told me.

I could hardly believe what I was hearing. I never expected that reaction! Those were the most healing words I had ever heard. He showed instantaneous love and forgiveness. We moved my things back in that week. When the final section of the divorce papers arrived in the mail, we ripped them up and threw them away.

Later, alone in my room, I knelt before God and confessed

in detail the names and places of every sin I could think of. The words "infidelity," "adultery," and others passed across my lips, and it was as if Jesus was scrubbing away my sins. God seemed to be saying, "You are finally here. I am so glad. I love you." It brought healing to my soul to communicate with my Lord again. I knew my shame was gone forever.

I was at work one day giving a presentation to a large group of businessmen. As I packed up after the class, one of the men gave me an entreating look. I glanced down at my attaché, and was relieved to remember: I did not have to smile back. I did not have to do anything at all. That was the old Julie.

More healing came throughout the next year of our marriage as God did a work of restoration. Peace and joy entered our home as it never had before. I understood and was relieved to realize that my worth was not measured by my abilities, or my appearance. It says in 1 Samuel: "For the Lord sees not as man sees; man looks on the outward appearance, but the Lord looks on the Heart."

One morning, standing with a warm cup of coffee in my hand, I gazed at a picture of my husband and me holding my little sister's newborn child. Cuddling this sweet life triggered nurturing, maternal thoughts in me. Treasuring the renewed love David and I shared, we decided to have our own baby. She came along the following year. When our precious daughter was born, we had a picture taken, this time with David and me, and our own little baby in the middle. With this gift of my precious daughter, I grasped true for-giveness; for I knew, I was more blessed than I could ever deserve.

ELEVEN
MARGARET HARRIS

The night was winding down. My husband and Perry had been working long hours to reconstruct an old organ and as the church organist, I rewarded them with a home cooked meal.

"Thank you for the great dinner! I haven't eaten that well in a long time," said Perry, a single man accustomed to his own sparse cooking.

"Oh, it was my pleasure," I answered, smiling as he went out the door. Just before he headed down the porch steps, he said, "You know, I wasn't sure I'd be welcome here. I was surprised by the invitation since I've been having an affair with your husband."

I stared at him in a stunned silence, unable to reply. In that moment, it all became clear to me. During the last few years, my husband had changed his behavior in strange ways that I was at a loss to explain. He had begun staying out late and coming home in the early hours of the morning with alcohol on his breath. He was always apologetic at first, blowing it off with excuses. "Oh, I was just out with the guys playing poker," or, "I just lost track of time." He would beg my forgiveness, promising that it would never happen again. I had no idea that this charming, blue-eyed chemistry major, who had stolen my heart and swept me off my feet, was now involved in a secret homosexual life.

Renne and I met while I was a junior at college. His engaging sense of humor and playful spirit attracted me right away, since I tended to lean toward the serious side of things. It was good for me, the daughter of an Episcopal priest, to feel the freedom to laugh and flirt with this handsome man. Yet it was not all play; we would sit for hours and discuss the meaning of life, as new couples are wont to do. I had become a Christian at a very young age and considered myself very spiritual, so occasionally, we enjoyed talking about God and the Bible. In the course of dating, Renne had independently decided to convert and become an Episcopalian. This, of course, pleased me. After my graduation, I started working in Boise and Renne continued his schooling in Indiana. That year, he came home for Christmas break and asked me to dinner.

"Margaret, you have captured my heart. I love who I am because of having you in my life" he said.

"I feel the same way. You've become so important to me," I answered.

He reached into his pocket and pulled out a little black box. "I love you. I want to spend the rest of my life with you. Will you marry me?"

Tears filled the corners of my eyes. This was my dream come true.

"Yes! Yes, I will absolutely marry you!"

We were married later that spring and moved to Indiana so that Renne could finish school. We had been married about six months when, for the first time, he came home drunk. It was not long before the drinking became a serious problem. Despite this, Renne attended church regularly and was very involved in our community. I remember a time once when we discussed sexuality, but I do not remember specifically talking about homosexuality. I did not really understand what he was trying to get across. It later became obvious that Renne was experiencing some urges that were difficult to sort through. However, at the time, I think Renee felt secure enough in our relationship and the love that we shared, to be protected from those urges he experienced.

Later, Renne had received his Master's degree in chemistry and was working on a Ph.D. when he decided that God was calling him into ministry. Although somewhat surprised, I was fully supportive of the decision. We agreed that he would get a job in his field so we could save enough money to move home to Oregon and be near family while he went to seminary. Shortly afterwards, Renne found a job in Portland, and we started our own family. It was a very stressful time because Renne continued to go out and get drunk often. He alternated between being very affectionate and loving toward me, to being verbally abusive. However, I tolerated, and even allowed, the abuse. Longing for it all to stop, I continued to pray for him to quit the excessive drinking and harsh talk. I could tell he did not want to hurt me, but there was something in his life hurting him. The only way he knew to handle it was to lash out.

Looking back, I have realized that we did not talk as openly as we should have. By nature, I am a "muller" and want to take time to sort out my thoughts before discussing them. Renne, on the other hand, was like a volcano. He would explode and then feel fine, while leaving the rest of us feeling terrible. It began to seem like I was married to two people. Most of the time, I still saw the fun-loving guy with the great sense of humor who liked to have a good time. Other times, he could not be pleased, regardless of my attempts. What really broke my heart, above all else, was that his violent outbursts usually occurred in front of our children. I remember once standing at the kitchen sink doing dishes. Renne was sitting at the table behind me and I could feel his frustration mounting.

"You have no idea what you're doing. Why do you do the dishes in such an unorganized, stupid way?" he barked.

"My way is fine, dear," I said defensively.

"No, it isn't! You're not doing it right," he said in a volume much too loud.

"Please, let me just finish and you won't have to worry..." I trailed off, for I was pushed out of my spot in front of the sink and watched as my husband drained the water and started the task over, showing me the *right* way to do the dishes.

"I don't see why it is necessary for me to do the dishes left to right instead of right to left," I said.

"You don't see why it's necessary? Oh, for goodness sakes, woman, stop arguing!" he bellowed.

Before I could even consider saying anything, an object came hurtling straight at me. Our toddler daughter playing in the next room looked up to see her mother duck out of the way and a plate crash against the wall, shattering glass everywhere.

Another conflict arose between us when Renne began to smoke pot regularly. I hated the smell and I did not like it in our house. He was still drinking a lot, and going out much more frequently, coming home later and later. Abusers are clever though. He knew exactly how to comfort me by saying things I wanted to hear. "You are the most beautiful woman in the world," or, "You are the most wonderful woman ever," and, "You have saved me from so much."

As much as I wanted to believe his words, it was extremely difficult to feel secure. Still, I trusted that I was in this marriage for keeps. I knew God was in it with us, and I sought His blessing.

Before long, Renne graduated seminary and was assigned to a church. He loved it. On Sundays he would go up to the pulpit to preach. Surprisingly, he was an incredible preacher. God used these sermons to console me every week and I was reminded that God could use anyone for His purposes. However, in spite of Renne being both my husband and my pastor, I could not tolerate his duplicitous lifestyle. I refused to sit back and let his secret consume him.

One night while I was in the kitchen cleaning up, Renne came stumbling in very late. "Oh, Margaret, I've made a mess of things. Do you remember how it used to be with us? Remember when we'd go on picnics and walks by the creek?" he slurred.

"Yes, I do. I wish it could be that way again," I sighed.

Suddenly, he fell off the stool and collapsed. He hit his head on the floor, hard. I could see he was beginning to panic. He screamed, "I can't move my body!" He could not move anything but his lips. I was very frightened and did not know what to do. After five minutes of paralysis, he recovered.

That was my wake up call. The next day I told him he had to get help and get sober or I would leave him. Renne agreed and went to an institution for two weeks. It was during those weeks that I learned Renne made pastoral rounds to parishioners. While visiting the ill and shut-ins, he would have a scotch (or two) at each house. I later learned he was making up to five "scotch house-calls" a day.

The psychiatrist he saw for the drinking problem thought that sexual preference was not something one could choose, nor could it be changed. Unfortunately, society agreed with her. There are myriad publications of literature to support that thinking, but I did not agree. I believed that God had called me to this marriage and He was to be the center of it. His intention was for a blessed union between a man and a woman. If I had not believed that principle, I would not have stuck it out as long as I did. Sadly, the doctor convinced Renne that he should divorce me and make himself happy.

Renne decided to wait until the spring to leave because he needed to get a different job to support us. We spent the year living together in the house, even sleeping in the same bed for a time, yet living separate lives. If a visitor were to see our bedroom, the façade would not have lasted. My side of the room was stacked with books on healing, and biographies of saints and great men and women of God. Across the room, Renne had tacked up a poster on the wall of "The Gay Men's Chorus" and played their music continuously. He read books about the history of gay priests and monks that confirmed his sinful beliefs. Even his physical appearance began to change; he moved differently, the timbre of his voice changed. I will never forget walking by the bedroom one day. Renne was sitting on the edge of the bed with no clothes on, talking on the phone. His legs crossed in an effeminate manner. He was gabbing away as giddily as a teenage girl. He turned to me and said in a voice I had never heard before, "I have him now and I will never let him go." I knew scripture. I knew that voice was not something a psychiatrist could handle.

I turned to a priest friend for solace. Father Gene counseled me from God's Word, not from the accepted philosophy of the world as the psychiatrist had. I found comfort in just talking to him. His wise words and Godly advice gave me the tools I needed to cope. We prayed together and sang at the top of our lungs, things that were un-Episcopalian, but God seemed to know that it was just what I needed at that time in my life. Father Gene also helped to comfort my children, reassuring them that we would be provided for and that I could care for them on my own.

The divorce was, like many, nasty. Though Renne was the one who wanted the divorce, once he was out of the house, he could not be bothered with the details. I was the one who handled the legal matters and the kids felt the tension. Renne seemed to have forgotten what it meant to be a parent. Of course, the children were distraught. Eventually, I had to have the locks changed on the house. Renne had made the choice to leave, and had to face the consequences of that decision. He was not acting responsibly in the least. Instead of finding a job that would support the family, he got a job working as a cook at a pie house. Teaching my piano students barely made enough to provide the necessities. Renne was supposed to be making the payments on the house and it was not until the bank started to foreclose that I realized he had not made any payments in over six months. I lost the house. At 45 years old, I found myself in the job market for the first time in my life. I had no experience, at least none that I could quantify on a resume. Temporary jobs came along for a bit, but we were very poor.

I was overwhelmed. I began to rail against and question God. "Why? Why? Was it me? Did I, in some way, *cause* Renne to become gay? Did he marry me because he saw me as masculine? Did I misunderstand what God wanted for me, for my marriage, for my family?" I knew, without hesitation, that God brought my children into this world for His purpose and He was in their lives. "But why were we made to suffer so much pain?" I cried. Desperate for healing, for the marriage to work out, for peace of heart, for healing of my soul, I lay on the floor and prayed to God. Overcome, I asked Him to take this burden because it was too much for me to carry alone. I prayed for Renne and for his healing. I prayed for our children. "God, show me what it is You want me to learn from this," I pleaded.

God truly began to surround me with support in the most unusual ways. I went to work for a small company where the person I worked most closely with was a pastor's wife. Her husband had written a book about a pastor who was confronted with having an extramarital affair. In that case, the pastor had repented, the church community prayed with him, and he received forgiveness. What was not included in the book was something she confided in me – the fact that the affair was with another man. This woman understood the pain I was going through. I began to have coffee with other women who held each other accountable in their Christian walk. Soon, I met another woman whose husband had been in sexual relationships with men. At last, someone who could truly identify with my pain! Through this group of women, the healing I so desperately sought was provided. It felt so good to know that I was not alone. There were others out there experiencing the same ache and turning to the same Comforter. This was the first time that the Lord used the fellowship of women in my life.

This led me to a period of thorough self-examination. I studied Mary's life and sought the meaning of femininity. I learned that women are able to minister to others in special ways and mothers most especially, because they hold their children's identities in their hearts. I learned to fight the enemy, Satan. Before this experience, I do not think I really believed there was an enemy. The Lord used Psalms 139 to help me conquer the severe anger I held within me. That passage affirmed to me that the Lord made me just as I am and He treasures me.

People urged me to turn to Him and I told God, "Okay, I'll give it a try." Really, there was no place else. God drove me into His hands. I learned to trust the Lord financially by tithing, giving the Lord part of my earnings, and reaped the benefits of God's promise that He would provide for all our needs. People I did not even know would send us notes telling us that God had laid us on their hearts and there would be a check for $500. God provided for us repeatedly. He taught me to wait upon His perfect timing. God also used my gifts and talents in the church. I became the Spiritual Director with an office and a paycheck. It seemed a natural step. Promoted to a pastoral assistant position, I had a visitation ministry and God even used me to lead others to Him. This was the time of deepest healing for me. I resumed playing the organ and directing choirs. Slowly, I learned to let go and not hurl the hurt back at the person who had caused it.

My growth was illustrated to me when I got a phone call from Renne. He had a question about claiming the children on his taxes. Renne was furious to learn that I had claimed them on my tax return, which was my right as their provider. Suddenly, I realized that we were back into the old behavior of his screaming and my defensiveness and I thought to myself, "I don't have to listen to this abuse. I don't have to subject myself to this. I don't have to argue with him. I gave up this hurt to the cross of Jesus." I gently hung up the phone while Renne was ranting. I had let him go. That was the first moment I really felt free of him.

It is often through teaching others that we learn the real lessons of our own lives. Leading others to Christ, and using His life and the lives of His prophets as examples, opened my own eyes about my testimony. I learned that God sometimes *allows* us to go through exceedingly terrible circumstances to draw us closer to Him. He reveals His intentions and His powerful love in His own perfect time. No one is responsible for the decisions or sins of others. God used all of my hurt, pain, and suffering to turn me into someone I never could have become on my own. My newfound strengths are now expressed in ministry, in music, in fellowship, and in discipleship. I now worship at a non-denominational church where I continue on a path of spiritual growth.

I learned to forgive Renne, because I now know that forgiveness is an act of will. When we decide to forgive, God grants us the grace to do it. Sometimes, when I am with my children, I see their dad's smile and his fun-loving nature. I see his sparkle in their eyes and I am glad.

TWELVE
ZOEANN COOK

Turning off the ignition and picking up my purse from the passenger seat of my red Toyota, I reached for the door handle with my left hand and realized I could not move. I was overwhelmed with fear.

Fear was not anything new to me. It had slowly started to influence my life six months earlier when I began a daily walking routine with my daughter. I was finding it more and more difficult to keep pace with her, as the distance we walked got shorter and shorter.

"I used to be able to clean my house in a single day," I told her that first morning. "Now, I feel exhausted all the time. It takes me a week to do what I used to do in one day."

"I really don't like the sound of that," my daughter said. "Please, Mom, you've got to see a doctor."

The symptoms continued to worsen and I knew she was right. Climbing the stairs drained me so much that I had to sit down on the bottom stair and scoot myself up one stair at a time to go to bed at night. One morning, I awoke with numbness in my thumb. I thought a spider bit me. Yet, over the following few weeks, the numbing and tingling took over my hand, my arm, and then, finally, the entire left side of my torso. Distressed, I went to see a doctor. He referred me to a neurologist.

"What's happening to me?" I asked. "I've never felt so afraid."

"I'm scheduling you for an MRI."

"An MRI? Is that really necessary? I'm afraid of closed spaces."

"I wouldn't schedule it if it wasn't absolutely necessary," he said gently. "You will be fine. By the way, make sure your health insurance doesn't lapse."

Those were dark days filled with fear. Yet, I often felt God's presence. I knew the MRI tube was going to be a challenge. Upon entering the tube, I was overcome with claustrophobia.

"Mrs. Cook, how are you doing?" the technician asked.

"I am so afraid," I cried. "I know God is with me, but this is so scary."

"Are you a Christian?" he asked.

"Yes," I said, softly.

"So am I," the technician said. "Let's pray together."

Tears of relief filled my eyes as his prayer comforted me.

"Holy God," he said. "Be with us right now. You are so big and we are so small. Be the Comforter for ZoeAnn. Give her the peace that passes understanding. Cover her with Your love and Your healing light. Amen."

God comforted me through the technician. He told me of his faith in Jesus Christ, bestowed words upon me of encouragement and prayers, and helped me receive the peace and courage I needed to get through my attack of claustrophobia.

Later that week, as I sat in my cube at work, the phone call came.

"Mrs. Cook?"

"Yes," I said.

"Your diagnosis is multiple sclerosis," the nurse proceeded. "The MRI results show visible sclerosis scar tissue on your spinal cord."

I could have fallen through a cement floor. As hard as it was to hear this news, the diagnosis was just the beginning. The consultation with my physician came next.

He explained that MS is a disease capable of destroying the nervous system and that it could result in partial or complete paralysis, blindness, and a whole list of other debilitating effects. His final words that day were, "ZoeAnn, if you have an episode of paralysis that lasts longer than 24 hours, call me. Then we can prescribe medication."

Twenty-four hours... paralysis... blindness... debilitating... wheel chairs... I know people with MS. I do not want this, God! No, I do not want this! The news that I have this disease, this MS, this multiple sclerosis, this is not real, it cannot be true!

And it didn't seem true...until the day I found myself sitting in my red Toyota outside my office building, unable to move. It was as if my limbs were no longer mine. There I was, all by myself, immobile and overwhelmed. Six months of fear turned into horrible reality right there. Suddenly, it was very real and very true. I had MS!

Tears streamed down my face and onto my cell phone as I struggled to call my husband, Steve. When he finally answered, I could hardly speak. Hysteria slurred my words and the tears would not stop coming. Somehow, Steve began to understand what was happening to me. Yet, when he tried to comfort me with his voice and with his words, he realized they were not enough. Then my wonderful husband realized that only God could fix this pain and he began to pray.

In my heart, I was taken back to a night many years ago when we were new Christians. Our oldest daughter, then almost 4 years old, sat on the arm of an old, green, overstuffed chair and played with a toy American flag. Little ones seem to put everything in their mouths, and so it was with Tracy. I can still hear her scream as she fell from the chair arm with that flag in her mouth and hit the family room floor. The flag impaled her deep in the back of her throat. We swept her into our arms, dislodged the dowel from the back of her bloody mouth, and rushed for the door. I saw the blood and the puncture wound, and I can still remember our fear!

"We have got to get her to the hospital, now," Steve said. Then he stopped, looked into my tear-filled eyes, and repeated aloud the thought that seemed trapped in his head, "Do they even know how to fix this?"

"I don't know," I replied. Together, we realized at the same time that only God could fix this. As we knelt and prayed, little Tracy miraculously stopped crying. The blood went away, and the hole in the back wall of her throat – the hole I had seen with my own eyes just minutes before – the hole from which I had dislodged the flag, was gone!

Today the same realization took place. We both understood that only God could fix my paralysis. Alone and trapped in my car, I was helpless. Tethered to my husband through the telephone, Steve prayed with me for over 20 minutes without any changes in my condition. Then slowly the paralysis subsided and I was able to move my arm and leg again.

However, I was not healed. Over the next few months, I had many more episodes like this one and I even began to believe I had the disease. Yet, God continued to provide temporary relief through

Steve's prayers.

Then my sister-in law, Linda, invited me to a class at her church – the topic was "Healing." It was impeccable timing. Through attending this class I came to understand that I could read God's Word, the Bible, as if I were taking a dose of medicine. I could take His encouragement two, three, four, or as many times per day as I needed it to keep me focused on His promises. It seems that this is the only medicine anyone cannot take too much of.

Doctors and people I knew with MS encouraged me to read pamphlets and literature about multiple sclerosis so I could become aware of what to expect, and learn strategies for living with it. Some-one even invited me to an MS support group. However, my husband and many others helped me understand that God did not want me to see myself as a person with MS, nor to embrace this as "*my* MS." The words we speak are vital to our health and well-being.

The exhaustion and tingling numbness I felt did not im-prove, but as I read the Bible, I found comfort and hope in the prom-ises of God. This is the best medicine and it is available to everyone. Steve and I decided to believe those promises and I put myself on regular doses of scriptural medicine. Over the next several months, every time I experienced an episode, I immediately called Steve and we prayed together until the immobility subsided. Sometimes it took 15 minutes, sometimes 30 minutes or longer, but never 24 hours. We saw these as attacks from Satan because he wants to harm us and ruin our lives. MS was his way of trying to control and destroy my life. By then, I was having weekly episodes. Every time an attack came, we prayed and allowed Jesus to take over the fight for us. We could not win, but He could!

Then one day at a special church service about nine months after the whole ordeal began, our pastor called three people forward by name. I was one of them. He prayed for each of us specifically, and when he got to me, he said a word that stuck in my mind. He said, "LIVE!" loudly and with authority. "LIVE!"

After he prayed a bit more for me, I returned to my seat. Physically, I did not feel any different. Even while the pastor prayed for me, I had not felt anything special take place. Nevertheless, after that healing prayer, I never had another episode of paralysis again! Although I continued to have symptoms for a time, God started a miraculous healing process that very day.

Gradually, my energy level increased. Soon I could walk, and even run up the stairs. I could clean my house in one day again. The tingling and numbness in my body receded just as it had come; first, it cleared from my mid-torso and chest, then my neck and shoulder, and finally left my arm and my hand. This happened in a slow progression until the only lingering numbness was in my fingers.

Sometimes I would question God, "Why do I still have the numbness in my fingers?" Every time I asked, He told me, "Yes, you are still having some symptoms, but believe in Me." He reminded me to review the promises in the Bible – it was my medicine. I read them to myself again and again. I trusted Him and thanked Him for all that He had done so far. Two years later, the last of the tingling left my fingertips. I have been completely symptom free for nearly five years now – God has indeed healed me!

AFTERWORD

I trust you have enjoyed reading these pages and I pray that these stories have sparked hope in your heart. The miracle of Christ working in the heart of faith, is without doubt the most life changing experience any individual can under go. I have discovered that God built people to live in a community where they can be encouraged, strengthened and honored. A community where questions can be answered, people can be given time to contemplate and loving one another is the greatest joy.

I want to extend to you a personal invitation to come and visit our community. Come and meet the people whose stories you have read. Come and meet many more people with similar stories. Come and join in this great adventure of living life from a completely different center and source.

We extend to you our open doors, our warm hearts and our joyous welcome.

Finally, if you would like to meet this Jesus who has done so many things in our lives please call us and let us talk to you. You can also consider the following and then pray the prayer at the end. Either way we do encourage you to give us a call and let us share your joy and walk together.

- Recognize that you are dying because of your sin.

Rom 6:23 "Work hard for sin your whole life and your pension is death. But God's gift is real life, eternal life, delivered by Jesus, our Master." THE MESSAGE

- Believe that God your Father loves you and wishes to give you a new heart …

Ezek 11:19 "I will give them singleness of heart and put a new spirit within them. I will take away their hearts of stone and give them tender hearts instead, …" NLT

- Believe that God your Father wishes to fill your new heart with His life …

2 Cor 5:17 "What this means is that those who become Christians become new persons. They are not the same anymore, for the old life is gone. A new life has begun!" NLT

- Believe that God your Father can transform your whole life through Jesus Christ.

Eph 4:22-24 " … take on an entirely new way of life — a God-fashioned life, 23 a life renewed from the inside 24 and working itself into your conduct as God accurately reproduces his character in you." THE MESSAGE

Prayer—

Lord Jesus, I recognize that my sin is killing me physically, emotionally and spiritually. I need You to give me a new heart so that Your life can come and fill me. I recognize I am a sinner and need to be forgiven so I can escape the judgment of loss of life. I believe Your blood has forgiven my sin and I receive your forgiveness. I welcome Your Holiness into my new heart. I give myself to You so You can begin to remake and transform me. Amen

Jess G. Strickland

LIVING HOPE FELLOWSHIP
3350 SW 182ND AVE.
ALOHA, OREGON
97006

503-649-4673

WWW.THISISHOPE.COM

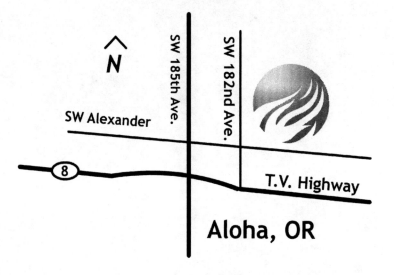

For more information on reaching your city with
stories from your church, please contact
Good Catch Publishing at...
www.goodcatchpublishing.com

GOOD CATCH
PUBLISHING